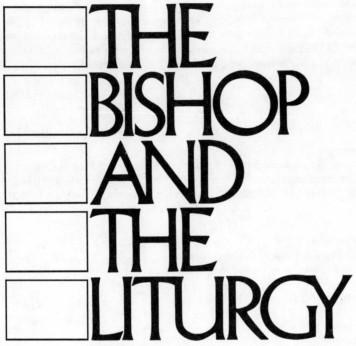

THE BISHOP AND THE LITURGY

Highlights of the
New Ceremonial
of Bishops

Secretariat
Bishops' Committee on the Liturgy
National Conference of Catholic Bishops

In its planning documents for 1985 and 1986, as approved by the National Conference of Catholic Bishops in November 1984 and in November 1985, the Secretariat of the Bishops' Committee on the Liturgy was authorized to commission and prepare a commentary on and excerpts from the *Caeremoniale Episcoporum* issued by the Congregation for Divine Worship. The final draft of the summary was reviewed and approved by Archbishop Daniel E. Pilarczyk, Chairman of the Bishops' Committee on the Liturgy, and is authorized for publication by the undersigned.

Monsignor Daniel F. Hoye
General Secretary
NCCB/USCC

April 18, 1986

On the Cover:
Illustrations are taken from an edition of *Pontificale Romano* published in 1520 in the city of Venice, contained in *Pontifical Services, Volume III, Illustrated from Woodcuts of the XVIth Century* (Alcuin Club collections VIII), with descriptive notes by F.C. Eeles (London: Longmans, Green & Co., 1907). The woodcuts illustrate, from top to bottom, the following pontifical rites:

Figure 1: Confirmation
Figure 2: Delivery of Gospel Book to Deacons
Figure 3: First Laying on of Hands, Ordination of a Priest
Figure 4: Delivery of Crozier, Ordination of a Bishop
Figure 5: The Oath, Blessing of an Abbess

Cover Design:
Al Porter Graphics
Washington, D.C.

BX
1971
.A25
1986

Typeface:
Times Roman

Typography:
WorldComp
Leesburg, Virginia

Excerpts from the English translation of *Documents on the Liturgy, 1963-1979: Conciliar, Papal, and Curial Texts* copyright © 1982, International Committee on English in the Liturgy, Inc. All rights reserved.

ISBN 1-55586-996-3

CONTENTS

FOREWORD

The recently published *Caeremoniale Episcoporum*, revised by decree of the Second Vatican Council to reflect the reformed Roman liturgy, replaces and abrogates the last edition published by decree of Pope Leo XIII in 1886.[1] The decree of promulgation by the Congregation for Divine Worship is dated 14 September 1984. Very soon after its publication, a second printing in 1985 incorporated a few changes and emendations.[2]

The *Ceremonial of Bishops* is not a liturgical book in the usual sense of that term, that is, a collection of rites for use in the celebration of the sacraments or other liturgical services of the Church. Rather, it is a book about the liturgy and how it is to be celebrated. The *Ceremonial of Bishops* is a collection of rubrics, directions, and guidelines whose purpose is to assist in the ordering of those celebrations over which the bishop presides.

The historical roots of the *Ceremonial* are found in the ancient *Ordines Romani* (especially *Ordo Romanus Primus*), books of directives and prayers that complemented the Sacramentaries of the Church of Rome.[3] While the Sacramentaries principally contained the prayers of the celebrant, the *Ordines* also contained the rubrical directives necessary to situate these prayers in the liturgical celebrations. But, ceremonial in the Roman Church was a sober affair, reflecting almost severe simplicity. While the Church in the East more freely adopted the ceremonial of the law courts, according the bishop the honors due a magistrate (e.g., incense, lights, etc.), up to the seventh century, ceremonial at Rome was essentially practical. Under the influence of the Carolingian Church, however, Roman liturgy underwent a ceremonial transformation. The restraint of Rome was augmented by the exuberance of the Franks and their love of ornamentation. Thus, the later *Ordines* exhibit a Frankish ceremonial influence which achieved its apogee in the thirteenth century.

---

[1] *Caeremoniale Episcoporum, ex decreto Sacrosancti Oecumenici Concilii Vaticani II insiaurai m auctoritate Ioannis Pauli PP. II promulgatum, editio typica*, Typis Polyglottis Vaticaris, MCMLXXXIV.

[2] See "Variationes in *Caeremoniale Episcoporum* inducendae," *Notitiae* 230-231 (September-October 1985): 494-495. Where necessary, the 1985 *variationes* have been incorporated into this book.

[3] For a historical overview of liturgical ceremonial, see Hugh Wybrew, "The Setting of Liturgy: Ceremonial" in *The Study of Liturgy*, C. Jones, G. Wainwright, E. Yarnold, SJ, editors (New York: Oxford University Press, 1978), 432-439.

By the time the *Pian Missal* was published in 1570, ceremonial in the Roman liturgy had begun to ebb into the undistinguished distinction of the two forms known to the Church before 1969: "low" and "solemn" or "high." This was especially true of the Mass. Oddly enough, the Low Mass became the practical and theoretical norm in the Roman Rite, relegating the Solemn or High Mass, with the participation of the various ministerial orders, to exceptional and very occasional circumstances. For, even though the High Mass was recommended for Sundays, holy days, and pontifical celebrations of the bishop, the Low Mass was the norm and influenced the carrying out of the more solemn form of the liturgy.

With the twentieth-century reform of the liturgy after the Second Vatican Council and the introduction of the principle of "progressive solemnity," ceremonial has once again taken its proper place in the liturgical life of the Church. The sung and fully participated Eucharist is enshrined as the norm in the *General Instruction of the Roman Missal* (1969; fourth edition, 1975). Liturgy that might be called "low" is seen as exceptional and quite secondary. Ceremonial is now based on the devout, active, and conscious participation of the entire community, ministers and assembly. Liturgy is expected to be musical, processions are obligatory. The use of lights and incense, vestments, beautiful vessels—all that enhances the environment for worship is to be planned and executed carefully and with reverent dignity. And, the liturgy over which the bishop, as promoter and guardian of worship in the local Church, presides is once again seen as the model and norm for all worship.

The new *Ceremonial of Bishops* represents a new stage in the revival and renewal of ceremony that is true to the origins of the Church's worship. It overturns the artificial distinction between "high" and "low" forms of worship and, for all practical purposes, continues the restoration of the principle and practice of full participation of the entire Church in the liturgy. If only for this reason, the new *Ceremonial of Bishops* is to be welcomed warmly as an important liturgical resource.

The revised *Ceremonial of Bishops* contains a general introduction that presents the theological and pastoral aspects of the bishop's liturgical celebrations, as well as some of the more practical principles that generally apply to episcopal liturgies. Of major importance is the section describing the "Stational Mass of the Bishop," which was previously referred to as the "Solemn Pontifical Mass." The Stational Mass is the most complete form of the eucharistic liturgy over which the bishop presides. It presumes the participation of all the ministerial orders and liturgical ministries of the Church, as well as the full, conscious, and active participation of the faithful. The remainder of the *Ceremonial of Bishops* contains sections on each of the sacraments, the Liturgy of the Hours, blessings, seasonal and festive celebrations, and the rites for the important liturgical moments in the life of a bishop.

In order to assist bishops and masters of ceremonies in familiarizing themselves with the new *Ceremonial*, this book provides a summary of the introductory general principles and outlines the Stational Mass of the bishop and some of the more important liturgical celebrations in the bishop's ministry. For the sake of clarity and completeness, a number of other documents pertaining to vesture, insignia, and other matters relating to bishops and prelates are included in Appendix II.[4]

Numbers in parentheses refer to the Latin edition of the *Caeremoniale Episcoporum*. Other material in parentheses is added by way of commentary and is not part of the original text. It should be understood that the translation of the *Caeremoniale Episcoporum* contained in this book is not the "official translation." That will be issued in its complete form by the International Commission on English in the Liturgy.

Although the *Ceremonial of Bishops* is by its nature rubrical, its intent is pastoral. Therefore, the *Ceremonial* demands a pastoral, and not a "rubricist," response. For, when the bishop is gathered at the altar with his presbyters, deacons, ministers, and the assembly of the faithful, there is the image and reality of the local Church at prayer. Such occasions deserve to be celebrated with dignity and with pastoral sensitivity and, above all, in a prayerful manner. For, as the "steward of the sacred mysteries" and the one charged with governing and promoting worship, "the bishop should ensure that in his diocese the liturgy, which is the common and public worship of the people of God, is celebrated with as much dignity as possible and with an aware, reverent, and fruitful participation by all, with the sacred minister presiding, and with the observance of the prescribed norms."[5] With the proper spirit of love for the liturgy and pastoral concern for God's people, the observance of liturgical norms by the bishop and his assistants is meant to foster good worship throughout the local Church.

It is the hope, therefore, of the Bishops' Committee on the Liturgy and its Secretariat that this book will serve as a useful introduction to the forthcoming publication of the *Ceremonial of Bishops*.

The Secretariat wishes to acknowledge with gratitude the assistance of the following persons in the preparation of this book: Msgr. Alan F. Detscher, Director of Worship of the Diocese of Bridgeport and Consultant to the Bishops' Committee on the Liturgy; Dr. Thomas C. O'Brien of the Secretariat of the International Commission on English in the Liturgy; Fr. Aidan Shea, OSB, of St. Anselm's Abbey, Washington, D.C.; and Sr. Ursula Infante, MSC, Cabrini College, Radnor, Pennsylvania. The Secretariat is also grateful to Msgr. Martimort for permission to reprint his article on the *Ceremonial of Bishops* from *Notitiae*. Finally, a special word of thanks to Archbishop Virgilio

---

[4]Translations by the International Commission on English in the Liturgy in *Documents on the Liturgy, 1963-1979: Conciliar, Papal, and Curial Texts* (Collegeville, Minn.: The Liturgical Press, 1982).

[5]Congregation of Bishops, *Ecclesiae imago, Directory on the Pastoral Ministry of Bishops* (22 February 1973), no. 80 (DOL 2650).

Noè, Secretary of the Congregation for Divine Worship, for permission to include his essay from *Notitiae* in this book and for his tireless efforts in seeing to the promulgation of the *Caeremoniale Episcoporum* in 1984.

	Reverend John A. Gurrieri
21 April 1986	Executive Director
Anselm, bishop and doctor	Secretariat
of the Church	Bishops' Committee on the Liturgy

THE NEW *CEREMONIAL OF BISHOPS**

Archbishop Virgilio Noè, Secretary
Congregation for Divine Worship

1. On 14 September 1984, the new *Caeremoniale Episcoporum,* promulgated by decree of the Congregation for Divine Worship, was published. This book had been long awaited by liturgists. Older bishops had felt the need of a sure guide for the celebration of the liturgy after Vatican II. Bishops called to the episcopacy after the liturgical reform also felt the need of a resource that would help them prepare for liturgical celebrations, which are so prominent and so important in a bishop's life. Masters of ceremonies also awaited a guide to assist them in the preparation and carrying out of the various rites. The newly published *Caeremoniale Episcoporum* has been warmly welcomed, as the many orders received for the volume concretely attest.

2. Consisting of nearly 400 pages, this handsome volume is bound in red cloth, with gold lettering. The first pages touch on some of the highlights of the history of the *Caeremoniale Episcoporum.* Of course, the four pages of the *Prooemium* cannot, nor do they intend to, give a complete history. But, they do outline the principal sources of the work, beginning with the end of the seventh century and concluding with the last edition of 1886, ordered by Pope Leo XIII (1878-1903). These prefatory pages mention the great figures who worked in this field: the anonymous authors of the *Ordines Romani* from the seventh to the fourteenth centuries; the great ceremonial experts of the Renaissance, such as Pietro Burgense in the time of Nicholas V (1448-1455), and Agostino Patrizi, Giovanni Burcardo, Paride de Grassi during the pontificates from Innocent VIII (1484-1492) to Leo X (1513-1521).

These men all worked on the papal liturgy, which in turn served as a model and guide for the liturgy in the cathedral churches of the Roman Rite throughout the world. During the years after the Council of Trent, at the suggestion of St. Charles Borromeo, a commission on rites was established by Gregory XIII (1572-1582). The commission, with Cardinal Gabriele Galeotti as president, was to prepare a book of ceremonies for bishops.

3. The desired ceremonial became a reality in 1600, when Clement VIII

---

*Virgilio Noè, "Il Nuovo *Caeremoniale Episcoporum,*" *Notitiae* 221 (December 1984): 953-957.

(1592-1605) published his *Caeremoniale Episcoporum,* which made ample use of the writings of Agostino Patrizi, Burcardo, Paride de Grassi, and many others. Preparation of the work had been entrusted to men noted for their knowledge and holiness who were then working for the Sacred Congregation of Rites: Cesare Baronio, Robert Bellarmine, and Silvio Antoniano. The work was intended for *omnibus ecclesiis praecipue autem metropolitanis, cathedralibus et collegiatis* and was recommended as *opus perutile et necessarium.* Clearly, this volume was well received, since between 1600 and 1886 there were thirteen Roman editions. There were also editions published in Venice, Turin, Paris, Malines, Ratisbon, Lyons, Cologne, Antwerp, and Frankfurt, each characterized by its own corrections, emendations, additions, index, and summaries. It is a very interesting chapter in liturgical publishing!

4. After the revision of nearly all the liturgical books in accord with the letter and spirit of Vatican Council II, a complete revision of the *Caeremoniale Episcoporum* became necessary, in order that, in keeping with the statement of the *Constitution on the Liturgy,* (art. 41), the bishop would be clearly seen as "the high priest of his flock, the faithful's life in Christ in some way deriving from and depending on him." The *iter instaurationis* of the volume, begun as early as 1964 by Study Group XXVI of the Consilium for the Implementation of the *Constitution on the Liturgy,* resulted in a draft by 1971 and reached the galley-proof stage by the end of 1975. But, the progress of the work became difficult and came to a complete standstill with the abolition of the Congregation for Divine Worship in July 1975. Work on the ceremonial was resumed in 1978 and profited from the comments made by the experts to whom the 1975 galley proofs had been submitted. The *Caeremoniale* was substantially ready by 1981, but it was decided to delay its publication until promulgation of the new Code of Canon Law and publication of *De Benedictionibus.* This delay was useful because it permitted taking into account the pertinent juridical and liturgical content of these two works.

Now that the new *Caeremoniale* has been published, it is a debt owed in gratitude to acknowledge those who worked on it, especially those who already take part fully in the heavenly liturgy (see *Constitution on the Liturgy,* art. 8). Above all, there is Archbishop Annibale Bugnini, first Secretary of the Congregation: to him is due the credit of proposing a revision of the ceremonial and of believing in its value, even when among some liturgists there was not only reluctance, but downright opposition to such a work. A second name to be mentioned is that of Msgr. Theodore Schnitzler, parish priest of Cologne. At the service of the revision of the *Caeremoniale,* he placed his experience as master of ceremonies in the cathedral of Cologne, his pastoral work in the parish of the Twelve Holy Apostles in Cologne, and his knowledge as professor of liturgy. His last years of collaboration with the Congregation were motivated by the desire to provide, by means of this book, what he regarded to be still lacking in the liturgical reform: care for the ceremonial side of liturgy. The third name to be mentioned is that of Msgr.

6

Salvatore Famoso of the Archdiocese of Catania. Until his death in 1982, work on the ceremonial continually benefited from his preciseness in the formulation of norms and from his attention to detail in the description of liturgical celebrations. He has left behind the memory of one who loved the liturgy and spent his life in its service.

5. The new *Caeremoniale Episcoporum* replaces and abrogates the former one, last published during the pontificate of Leo XIII in 1886. The norms of the new work have as their purpose to make possible a liturgy that is marked by a noble simplicity, that is pastorally effective, and that is adapted to the understanding of the faithful. At the same time, these requirements must be in harmony with the demands of the *pietas et reverentia* due to a bishop, in whose person Jesus Christ is present in the midst of the believers as the eternal shepherd (*Dogmatic Constitution on the Church*, 21).

6. The book has eight parts. The first presents the theology of the local Church and of celebrations of the liturgy under the presidency of the bishop and with the participation of his presbyters, of deacons, other ministers, and of the people entrusted to his care. Part I also includes general norms on vestments and pontifical insignia and on signs of reverence to be used in celebrations. Part II deals with Masses at which a bishop presides; Part III, with celebration of the Liturgy of the Hours; Part IV, with the celebrations belonging to the cycle of the liturgical year. Parts V and VI present, respectively, the liturgies of the sacraments and sacramentals at which a bishop presides. Part VII speaks of the same material in a more particular manner, as it describes the most important days in a bishop's life: his election for ordination; his taking possession of the diocese at his first entrance into the cathedral; even his death and funeral. The last part, Part VIII, treats celebrations connected with acts of a bishop's pastoral government, such as synods, pastoral visitations, installation of a new pastor in a parish. The three appendices deal with the vestments of prelates; the order of precedence of liturgical days; and ritual Masses, Masses for various needs, votive Masses, and Masses for the dead. An eighty-page *Index rerum notabilium* facilitates access to the contents of the *Caeremoniale*.

7. A great deal of current liturgical legislation has been integrated into the *Caeremoniale*, where it has a new context and character. Norms incorporated from the earlier liturgical books retain the same obligatory force they have in their source. Wherever the *Caeremoniale* presents changes of liturgical norms, these norms as given in the *Caeremoniale* are to be followed.

8. The new *Caeremoniale* is a book intended for bishops, masters of ceremonies, and all priests who love beautiful and orderly liturgies. It is a practical book, as is clear, for example, from the *descriptio ritus*, which indicates the order in which each rite is arranged, and from the *quae parentur*, that is, the list of things to be prepared for each celebration. It is a spiritual book. It indicates to the director of a liturgy the right spiritual viewpoint for each celebration that will ensure that all who take part in any way will receive

the spiritual effect of the celebration. It is a pastoral book. Its purpose is to lead all those involved in a celebration to consider it and to experience it, not as an external performance, but as a principal manifestation of the local Church.

9. In the *Caeremoniale Episcoporum*, no one is mentioned as often as the bishop. It is he who presides *in persona Christi*. Many years before the Council, in the days of Msgr. Carinci, Secretary of the Congregation of Rites, a reform of the *Caeremoniale* was envisioned. Receiving the members of the commission responsible, the then *substitutus* of the Secretariat of State, Msgr. Giovanni Battista Montini, included in his remarks this thought: "It is necessary to give bishops the honors they deserve, without forgetting that the principal person in the liturgical drama is our Lord himself." Such is the spirit that pervades the new *Caeremoniale Episcoporum*.

FEATURES OF THE
*CAEREMONIALE EPISCOPORUM**

A. G. Martimort, Consultor
Congregation for Divine Worship

After its establishment in 1964, the Consilium for the Implementation of the *Constitution on the Liturgy* charged *Coetus* XXVI (Study Group 26) with the task of preparing the *Caeremoniale Episcoporum*. I was appointed the group's *relator*, and Salesian Father Armando Cuva was named secretary. The following experts worked with the *coetus*: Msgr. Joaquim Nabuco of Brazil, author of works on the *Pontificale* and the *Caeremoniale;* Msgr. Pietro Borella, historian of the Ambrosian liturgy and master of ceremonies in the Cathedral of Milan; Msgr. Giovanni Schiavon, master of ceremonies in the Cathedral of Venice; Msgr. Salvatore Famoso, master of ceremonies in the Cathedral of Catania. They benefited repeatedly from the help of Dom Raphael Hombach, the Abbey of Maria-Laach; Fr. Carlo Braga, CM; and Msgr. Imanuel Bonet, vice-dean of the Tribunal of the Rota. After a certain number of work sessions, the first of which took place on 15 December 1964, the group was in a position to have the Fathers of the Consilium[1] approve, on 1 December 1965, a first series of decisions aimed at simplifying the ceremonial of liturgical services presided over by the bishop and at applying the wish expressed by the Council[2] to reserve the use of pontifical insignia to bishops and to those who possess some definite jurisdiction.

After the necessary contacts with the various interested agencies of the Curia, these decisions were promulgated on 21 June 1968, in two distinct documents.

1. The one, which required the personal authority of the pope and which, therefore, took the form of a *Motu proprio*, beginning with the words *Pontificalia insignia*, suppressed, but not retroactively, all the privileges of pontifical insignia granted to ecclesiastics who are not bishops and

---

*A. G. Martimort, "Le Cérémonial des Eveques," *Notitiae* 225 (April 1985): 196-206.
[1] Consilium Schema 128.
[2] Second Vatican Ecumenical Council, Constitution on the Sacred Liturgy, *Sacrosanctum Concilium* (= SC), art. 130.

who do not have true jurisdiction in the external forum. Those who have such jurisdiction would be able to use pontifical insignia only in their own territory and for the duration of this jurisdiction. There were particular provisions in favor of abbots within monasteries of their order.[3] A more radical step was taken later, 30 October 1970, by the Congregation for the Clergy, according to the instructions that it had received from the Cardinal Secretary of State.[4] This letter of the Congregation abolished all past privileges and henceforth forbade use of all pontifical insignia by canons.[5]

2. The second document, *Pontificalis ritus,* was an instruction issued by the Congregation of Rites, signed by Cardinal Benno Gut in his twofold capacity as Prefect of the Congregation and President of the *Consilium,* and countersigned by Fr. Ferdinand Antonelli, OFM, Secretary of the Congregation.[6] This document aimed at bringing to the *Caeremoniale Episcoporum* both those adaptations required by the newly restored rite

to simplify the rites by suppressing elements that suggested the etiquette of the princely courts of the Renaissance, for example, the vesting of the bishop at the chair or the *pregustatio* [the sampling of the wine beforehand to determine both its validity as matter and to ascertain that it was not poisoned], and other useless complications pertaining to vesture and ceremony. When the bishop presides at the Mass without celebrating it, instead of "holding chapel" [*tenir chapelle,* in French][7] as formerly, he is to carry out himself whatever pertains to the celebrant in the Liturgy of the Word. Every bishop, even one without local jurisdiction, is always to officiate at the *cathedra,* which is reserved to him.

These several norms were the only ones that could be issued at that time: the ritual of ordinations was only published two months later; the *Ordo Missae,* the rites for the baptism of children, marriage, and funerals would appear only in 1969; the consecration to a life of virginity and the blessing of abbots

---

[3]Reiner Kaczynski, *Enchiridion Documentorum Instaurationis Liturgicae* (= EDIL) 1089-1098; see also *Documents on the Liturgy, 1963-1979: Conciliar, Papal, and Curial Texts* (= DOL) 4447-4456.

[4]Instruction *Ut sive sollicite* of 31 March 1969, n. 35: EDIL 1361; DOL 4497-4532.

[5]Circular Letter of the Congregation for the Clergy, 30 October 1970, nos. 1-4: EDIL 2190-2195; DOL 4533-4537.

[6]6. See EDIL 1099-1138; DOL 4457-4496.

[7]*Tenir chapelle* refers to the earlier requirement that the bishop, sitting upon the throne, be vested in cope, assisted by two deacons. So vested and from the throne, the bishop would lead the *Confiteor,* give the ministerial blessings and the final apostolic blessing to the faithful.

in 1970; *The Liturgy of the Hours*, the consecration of holy oils, and confirmation in 1971. Not until November 1970, then, was it possible to envisage undertaking the revision of the *Caeremoniale Episcoporum*.

Direction of this work was entrusted to Msgr. Theodor Schnitzler, the true author, who, by his competence and exquisite cordiality, encouraged his small group of collaborators: Msgr. Noè, Undersecretary of the Congregation for Divine Worship and, since the previous 7 January, master of papal ceremonies; Don Piero Marini, on staff at the Congregation, after having worked on the *Consilium*; and, finally, myself. At various stages, Msgr. Famoso, mentioned earlier, and Canon Jose Antonio Cavada de la Riva of Madrid joined this enterprise. Intensive work sessions took place at Vicarello (7-12 May 1971) and, above all, at Cologne, where we enjoyed the delightful hospitality of Msgr. Schnitzler and his sister at the presbytery of the Basilica of the Holy Apostles (3-7 January, 25 June to 1 July 1972; 2-9 January 1973; 17-20 June 1975; 8-15 February 1977).

A first partial draft was submitted to the *Consulta* of the Congregation on 18 February 1972. Later, a version *pro manuscripto* was sent on 21 April 1975 to all the bishops, in order to invite their observations. The review of these observations led to improvement of the text, which was ready for final printing at the beginning of 1978. But, by this time, the Congregation for Divine Worship had been given the status of a section of the Congregation for the Sacraments and had to cope with the problem of too much work and a reduced staff. This explains why the publication of the *Caeremoniale* was only possible in September 1984.

The new *Caeremoniale* does not intend, any more than did the former one, to derogate from local customs, provided that they are in conformity with the spirit of the Constitution *Sacrosanctum Concilium* (= SC) of Vatican Council II. Besides, most of the prescriptions that it contains derive their force from the liturgical books that had been already published. Nevertheless, the new *Caeremoniale* does present changes in some cases: during its editing it was possible to bring uniformity to rubrics that, because they had been edited over a ten-year period, differed in formulation from rite to rite. In some cases, as well, the arrangement and process of the rites have been improved.

The *Caeremoniale* is divided into eight parts of unequal length. Part I, *De liturgia episcopali in genere* ("Episcopal Liturgy in General"), first establishes, in the light of the Constitution *Lumen Gentium* (= LG), the theological foundations of a liturgy at which the bishop presides. The liturgy should be the preeminent manifestation of the proper character of the local Church by means of "the full and active participation of all the people of God in the same celebrations, above all in the Eucharist, in a single prayer, at the one altar at which the bishop surrounded by his priests and his ministers presides" (SC, 41). This statement refers not to pomp, etiquette, or mere ceremony, but to the organic character of the Church. Thus, breaking with the style of the former *Caeremoniale*, the new text rediscovers, so to speak, the thought of Saint Ignatius of Antioch or of Saint Cyprian, in order to present successively the proper role of the bishop, the place of the priests around him, the functions of other ministers. Then, it describes what the structure of today's cathedral church should be, in order to permit the carrying out of the renewed rites and to be a visible representation of the makeup of the diocesan community.

The editing of the chapter in Part I entitled *De quisbusdam normis generalioribus* ("Some General Norms") required balanced judgment, in order to achieve harmony between the contemporary "noble simplicity" intended by Vatican II (SC, 34) and other considerations. Among these are the requisite marks of respect inspired by the spirit of faith that sees in the bishop the presence of Jesus Christ in the midst of believers (LG, 21) and these "mutual signs of honor" with which the members of the Mystical Body ought "to outdo ~ne another" (Rom 12:10). The former excesses of a triumphalistic protocol 'e given way to the opposite extreme, of an easygoing nonchalance and ̖areless familiarity. The aim of this chapter of the *Caeremoniale* is to provide a proper balance by describing what the vestments and insignia of a bishop should be, in view of both tradition and present-day attitudes; the marks of respect due to the Blessed Sacrament, the altar, the *Book of the Gospels*, the bishop himself; the rules pertaining to incensation, the sign of peace, the use of holy water, and the various liturgical gestures.

We should also call attention to several happy improvements in this chapter of the liturgical books published previously. The following in particular may be mentioned. "The bishop is at all times to wear the episcopal ring, the symbol of his faith and of his union with the Church his Spouse" (no. 58). Therefore, he is to wear it on Good Friday, contrary to a questionable rubric in the *Ritus pontificalis hebdomadae sanctae* ("Pontifical Rite for Holy Week"), which by an oversight is mistakenly repeated in no. 315 of the *Caeremoniale* itself; the ring is not to be regarded as a piece of jewelry, but as a symbol of the bishop's bond with the Church. It is also noteworthy that in allowing another bishop to preside at a celebration the diocesan bishop thereby grants him the right to use the crosier (no. 59). The crosier is used henceforth even in the offices of the dead (nos. 822-836). In indicating when the mitre is to be worn, the new *Caeremoniale* eases the rules with the phrase "as a rule" (*de more;* no. 60). On the other hand, the *Caeremoniale* rightly corrects *De Ordinatione* (Rite of Ordination) by reestablishing the traditional usage according to which the bishop wears the mitre "when carrying out ritual gestures pertaining to the sacraments" (nos. 60, 509, 582). The use of the pallium by a metropolitan is no longer limited to certain specific feast days but is now governed by a more general rule (no. 62).

Part II, *De Missa* ("The Mass"), is particularly important and will have to be studied with care. The *General Instruction of the Roman Missal* seems to disregard the Mass celebrated by the bishop. Great historians of the liturgy like Duchesne and Battifol would have sharply criticized this lacuna; they were rightly of the opinion that the rites of the Mass had as their paradigm the celebration by the bishop and not, as in the rubrics of the *Missal of St. Pius V*, the private celebration of the Mass. For this reason, the description of the Mass in the new *Caeremoniale* provides many clarifications and, in some cases, modifications of the *General Instruction*.

Even more noteworthy is the change of focus that guides the description of the Mass in Part II. No longer is there reference to the "pontifical Mass" or a "solemn Mass"; the emphasis is on the "Stational Mass." What justifies the particular rules of this Mass is not the need to "solemnize" a feast or to surround the bishop with special signs of rank. Rather, it is the fact that the entire local Church, clergy and faithful—or at least their representatives—is called to the Mass of the bishop. That is what is envisioned by the term *statio* (station), borrowed from the vocabulary of the sacramentaries and the Roman *ordines*. (Fr. Josef Jungmann had proposed the title *Statio orbis* for the 1960 International Eucharistic Congress in Munich.) The Stational Mass of the bishop ought then to manifest both the unity of the local Church and the variety of ministries exercised around the bishop and the Eucharist (no. 19). This Mass no longer specifies a fixed and limited number of ministers; rather, it invites all priests to concelebrate with their bishop (even if, for pastoral reasons, they have already celebrated Mass that day). The Stational Mass also invites all the deacons—and at least three—to exercise their ministry and calls for the participation of duly instituted lay ministers. It goes without saying that the integrity of ministerial functions is to be strictly observed: "In liturgical celebrations each one, minister or layperson, who has an office to perform, should do all of, but only, those parts which pertain to that office by the nature of the rite and the principles of liturgy" (SC, 28). Thus, for example, the practice of priests vesting as deacons should disappear.[8] Canons who do not concelebrate are no longer to be vested but are to wear choir vesture (no. 123).

The vesting of the bishop no longer takes place in choir, as the former ceremonial allowed in imitation of the princely courts, but rather it takes place, according to ancient tradition, in the *secretarium*, a room or chapel set aside for this purpose and from which the entrance procession begins (nos. 53, 126).

Ideally, the cross and the candlesticks, normally seven in keeping with Revelation 1:13–2:1, that are carried in the procession are those that also will serve as the cross and candlesticks placed around the altar (no. 129).

The dignity of the *Book of the Gospels* is to be emphasized. Normally distinct from the Lectionary, this book is carried by one of the deacons in the entrance procession and placed by him in the middle of the altar (but, no. 131 has overlooked the fact that the bishop is to kiss the *Book of the Gospels*

---

[8]What, then, is to be thought of the practice in which cardinals, who have received episcopal ordination, are nevertheless vested, at times, in the diaconal dalmatic in certain papal ceremonies?

after having kissed the altar when he reaches it). To avoid interrupting the gospel procession, the deacon goes to the bishop for the blessing before going to take the book from the altar to the lectern (no. 140). As is fitting, after the deacon has proclaimed the Gospel he brings the book for the bishop himself to kiss (no. 141).

The following rubric is both sensible and practical: "Care should be taken that the incensation has been completed before the *Orate, fratres* and the prayer over the gifts are said" (no. 149).

In the course of describing the way the Mass proceeds, the *Caeremoniale* also indicates the points at which, according to circumstances, other rites are inserted: the sprinkling of holy water on Sunday, the consecration or blessing of persons, the blessing of the oils of the sick. Such directives will be appreciated by masters of ceremonies.

The final blessing is given by the bishop according to one of the solemn modes indicated by the *Missal* and the *Pontifical;* but, as an alternative to the usual formulary, given in no. 1121, the bishop may use the formulary provided in no. 1120:

> The bishop takes the mitre, if one is is being used, and, with hands outstretched, greets the people, saying, "The Lord be with you," to which all respond, "And also with you." Then the bishop, with hands outstretched over the faithful, continues, "May the peace of God, which surpasses all understanding, keep your hearts and your minds in the knowledge and love of God and of his Son, our Lord, Jesus Christ." All respond, "Amen." Then the bishop, having taken the crozier, if it is being used, says, "May almighty God bless you," and, making the sign of the cross over the people, adds, " + the Father, + and the Son, + and the Holy Spirit."

In all cases, the sign of the cross is made but once, although this is not said explicitly (no. 169).[9] We should also point out the new rite of papal blessing (nos. 1122-1126); this is coordinated with the relevant parts of the Mass, the penitential rite, the general intercessions, and the final blessing, which it replaces with its own, proper formulary.

Finally, Part II of the new *Caeremoniale* briefly indicates the manner in which the bishop celebrates a Mass other than the Stational Mass; it is always to be clear that he is the high priest of his flock (nos. 171-174). The rules, issued in 1968, on the bishop's presiding at a Mass in which he himself is not the celebrant, are repeated in nos. 175-186.

Part III, *De Liturgia Horarum et de celebratione verbi Dei,* concerns the Liturgy of the Hours and celebrations of the Word of God. The same

---

[9]But, the 1985 reprinting of the *Caeremoniale Episcoporum* restores the triple benediction by adding the word *ter* (see no. 169).

entrance procession as at Mass is indicated for the celebration of Morning Prayer and Evening Prayer on great solemnities. Upon both his entrance and departure the bishop goes to the altar to kiss it, a traditional gesture of reverence all too often forgotten (no. 196). The hymn, the antiphons, the psalms are no longer, as formerly, intoned by dignitaries but by the cantors, a procedure that fosters the quiet and meditative execution of the psalmody. Provision is made (no. 198) for the bishop-celebrant to say the psalm-prayer, described in the *General Instruction of the Liturgy of the Hours*, no. 112 (the formulary of such psalm-prayers has yet to be published).[10]

Regrettably, if I may say so, the *General Instruction of the Liturgy of the Hours* and the new *Caeremoniale* continue the ritual of incensation of the altar and of persons during the Canticle of Mary and the Canticle of Zechariah; this ceremony (not to mention the organ interludes occasioned by the length of the incensation) is a distraction from the singing of the canticles. The incensation stems from a historical misinterpretation. Originally, the incensation did not accompany the *Magnificat*, but rather the singing of the preceding *Dirigatur* (which survived only as a versicle at Evening Prayer of Sundays in Ordinary Time). Thus, the incensation was at one time an evening rite, *sacrificium vespertinum*. Today, it would be much better linked, as in the Ambrosian liturgy, to the veneration of the altar at the beginning of Evening Prayer. There is no reason whatever for keeping this rite in Morning Prayer, where it was incorporated simply for reasons of symmetry with Evening Prayer.

Part IV, *De celebrationibus mysteriorum Domini per anni circulum* ("Celebrations of the Mysteries of the Lord during the Cycle of the Year"), has the merit of being a useful development of the *General Norms for the Liturgical Year and the Calendar*, which is printed in the *Sacramentary* after the *General Instruction of the Roman Missal*. There is a brief but worthwhile catechesis at the beginning of each chapter on the meaning of the feast or the celebration. For each one of these celebrations, the list of articles to be prepared is provided, and this will facilitate the work of sacristans.

The following are worthy of special mention: the rites for Christmas eve (no. 238); a resume of the steps in Christian initiation, normally celebrated during Lent (no. 250); the encouragement—perhaps antiquarian—to organize "stations" during Lent, that is, pilgrimages from one church to another in the city, in imitation of the ancient Roman practice (nos. 260-262); the detailed description of the Chrism Mass (nos. 274-279), including the priests' renewal of their promises (no. 280); the complete plan of the Paschal Vigil, including the celebration of the sacraments of initiation (nos. 337-370); a chapter recalling the nature and characteristics of the Easter season (nos. 371-376); another chapter on the significance of the Sundays in Ordinary Time (nos. 377-380). Following the conciliar Constitution, there is a reminder that it is

---

[10]The ICEL text of *The Liturgy of the Hours* does include such psalm-prayers in the psalter.

the responsibility of the conference of bishops in each region to establish, on dates that correspond to the climate, celebrations replacing the former Rogation Days and Ember Days (nos. 381-384).

The new *Caeremoniale* clearly separates the description of the sacramental rites, which are covered in Part V, from that of the sacramentals, which are the topic of Part VI. All these rites have been issued in their own separate typical editions; with the exception of the rites of ordination, which appeared first, these editions include rubrics in the *praenotanda* and within the text. In the *Caeremoniale*, such rubrics have, for the first time, been gathered together, an arrangement that points to the need to harmonize rubrics by giving identical rules concerning, for example, formularies used in ritual Masses,[11] readings, general intercessions, the profession of faith.

Moreover, the original editions of certain rituals made no provision for celebrations by the bishop himself; the clarifications on this matter will be welcome. In particular, the *Caeremoniale* recalls and revives the Roman tradition in which certain rites are carried out not by the bishop himself but by the priests assisting him, for example, in the celebration of baptism (nos. 365, 427, 436, 444, 451).[12] Similarly, the chapter *De Sacramento Ordinis* provides a complete description of the rites of ordination within Mass, a description lacking in the 1968 *Pontifical*.[13] At the ordination of a bishop in his own diocese (and not necessarily in his own cathedral), provision is made, in accord with the new Code of Canon Law (= CIC), for the presentation of his apostolic letter to the college of consultors in the presence of the chancellor of the diocesan curia (no. 573; CIC, c. 382.3). If the bishop-elect is a metropolitan and is to receive the pallium, the principal consecrator first puts the pallium on the bishop-elect before also putting on the mitre (no. 588). In the chapter on the sacrament of penance, it is rather surprising to find a rite for confession and general absolution: it is questionable that the case anticipated in CIC, c. 961.1,1 will ever, except perhaps in mission countries, occasion the need for a ceremonial presided over by the bishop assisted by a deacon (nos. 633-639). Besides, these numbers should have made express mention of the reminder of the obligation of later individual confession (CIC, cc. 962-963).

Part VI, *De sacramentalibus* ("Sacramentals"), following in each section the same arrangement of contents, provides for the blessing of abbots and abbesses; consecration to a life of virginity; perpetual profession of religious; institution of readers and acolytes; the bishop's presiding at funerals; the blessing of the cornerstone of a church; the dedication of a church and an altar; the blessing of a chalice and paten, a baptismal font, a cross, a bell,

---

[11]Cf. the Table (Appendix III) on p. 292.
[12]In another connection, see no. 602 on the celebration of marriage.
[13]See, however, the ICEL edition of the *Roman Pontifical* of 1978, in use in the English-speaking world.

and a cemetery. The inclusion, in this part, of the rubrics of the "Order for the Crowning of an Image of the Blessed Virgin Mary" (nos. 1033-1053) seems to me a vestige of preconciliar usage. We should also mention the rite that replaces the former "Reconciliation of a Violated Church," which is henceforth entitled *Publica supplicatio cum gravis iniuria ecclesiae est illata* (nos. 1070-1092).

Finally, Part VI also provides general rules for processions, eucharistic exposition and benediction, and, deserving of particular attention, a chapter entitled *De benedictionibus ab Episcopo impertiendis* ("Blessings to Be Given by the Bishop"), which, as we have already mentioned, provides a welcome revision of the formularies for the episcopal blessing and the papal blessing; neither of these had been included in any of the revised liturgical books.

Part VII, *De notabilibus diebus in vita Episcopi* ("Notable Days in the Life of a Bishop"), briefly lists the things a bishop-elect must do once he has been informed of his nomination; it then treats the time and place of his ordination, his taking possession of the diocese, and, if the ordination has taken place elsewhere, his reception at the cathedral; the ceremony of the imposition of the pallium on a new metropolitan. The new formulary for this last rite (no. 1154) replaces a medieval text that is out of keeping with the ecclesiology of Vatican II.

Finally, Part VII deals with the rites that should be celebrated upon the death and funeral of a bishop; the prayer during the vacancy of the see; the anniversaries that, by an ancient tradition, ought to be celebrated: the anniversary of the episcopal ordination of the diocesan bishop (St. Augustine and St. Leo the Great used to preach *in natali sui* before their assembled flock); the anniversary of the death of the bishop's predecessor.

Part VIII, which is also very brief, treats the rites for a plenary or provincial council and for a diocesan synod. I think it regrettable that, to my knowledge, no extant book preserves the ancient formularies of the old *Pontifical*, some of which are of Visigothic origin.[14] Part VIII also includes a ritual for the bishop's pastoral visit and a ritual for the installation of pastors, the second being a novelty in Roman books since hitherto only diocesan or regional rituals had included such a rite.

In its three appendices, the new *Caeremoniale* recapitulates the norms of 1969 and 1970 on the vesture of prelates; the table of precedence of liturgical days; and a very useful table outlining the rules governing ritual Masses, votive Masses, Masses for the dead. Finally, it is gratifying to find a hundred or so pages of index, which permits quick access to this or that rite or formulary.

This book will certainly be welcomed and will find its deserved place in all cathedral sacristies, as well as in the libraries of masters of ceremonies. We must thank, above all, the perseverance and deep spirituality of Msgr.

---

[14]C. Munier, "L'Ordo de celebrando concilio wisigothique," in *Revue des Sciences Religieuses* 37 (1963): 250-271.

Schnitzler, without whom his collaborators would not have had the courage to undertake the preparation of the work or would have given up in the face of its difficulties.

If the liturgical services presided over by the bishop are carried out according to the spirit of the new *Caeremoniale*, the faithful who participate will find in these liturgies one of the aspects of the mystery of the Church that Vatican II has emphasized: "Bishops individually are a visible principle and foundation of unity in their particular Churches, which are formed in the image of the universal Church, and in them and from them the one, unique Catholic Church has its being" (LG, 23).

I.

THE NATURE AND IMPORTANCE OF
EPISCOPAL LITURGY

1. The *Ceremonial* (no. 1) introduces the nature and importance of "episcopal liturgy," what was once termed "pontifical liturgy," by describing the diocese, the local or particular church over which the bishop presides: "A diocese is that portion of God's people which is entrusted to a bishop to be shepherded by him with the cooperation of the presbytery. Adhering thus to its pastor and gathered together by him in the Holy Spirit through the Gospel and the Eucharist, this portion constitutes a particular church in which the one, holy, catholic, and apostolic Church of Christ is truly present and operative."[1] And, as St. Ignatius of Antioch stated, "Where the bishop is, there should be the congregation, just as where Christ Jesus is, there is the Catholic Church."[2]

2. The bishop is at the heart of the Church for he represents and symbolizes Christ himself. The *Directory on the Pastoral Ministry of Bishops* (*Ecclesiae imago* = EI), issued on 22 February 1973, states that the "bishop exists as a living sign of Christ's presence in his Church, as one bearing witness to the Word of God and communicating God's life through the sacraments" (no. 16). Because the bishop is a sign and instrument of Christ, the eternal High Priest, the life of the faithful in Christ "in some way derives and depends on him" (SC art. 41/DOL 1,41). The bishop offers visible witness to the presence of Christ in the Church by his own presidency and participation in the liturgy, "showing the way by his own example" (EI 77/DOL 2647). The bishop is called to carry out the liturgical rites of the Church with "devoutness and gravity" (EI 78). Moreover, through prayer and worship "the bishop pours out upon the faithful in many ways and in abundance the fullness of Christ's holiness and stirs their resolve to strive, all in their separate ways of life, for Christian perfection" (EI 79).[3]

3. For these reasons, the role of the bishop in the liturgy is paramount, whether in the cathedral or in other churches of his diocese. "The bishop should ensure that in his diocese the liturgy, which is the common and public

---

[1] *Directory on the Pastoral Ministry of Bishops,* no. 11.
[2] St. Ignatius of Antioch, *Ad Smyrnaeos* 8,2; ed/Funk I, p. 283.
[3] See Paul VI on *communio* and the local church in DOL 499-502.

worship of the people of God, is celebrated with as much dignity as possible and with an aware, reverent, and fruitful participation by all" (EI 80). The bishop and those who work with him on a diocesan level therefore are to be aware of the provisions of the *Directory on the Pastoral Ministry of Bishops*, the various liturgical books, and the new *Ceremonial of Bishops* so that the bishop can fulfill his sanctifying office in the local Church.

4. Both the *Directory* and the *Ceremonial* place greatest emphasis upon liturgical celebrations in the cathedral, "the mother and teacher of the other churches of the diocese" (EI 81), and upon the "Stational Mass" and other liturgical celebrations, especially on the occasion of pastoral visitations.[4]

---

[4]See *The Cathedral: A Reader* (Washington, D.C.: United States Catholic Conference, Office of Publishing and Promotion Services, 1979), pp. 17-24.

II.

OFFICES AND MINISTRIES IN
EPISCOPAL LITURGIES

Bishops

5. "Any community of the altar, under the sacred ministry of the bishop, stands out clearly as a symbol of that charity and 'unity of the Mystical Body, without which there can be no salvation'" (*Dogmatic Constitution on the Church,* 26).

6. Since the bishop is marked with the fullness of the sacrament of orders, it is most appropriate that he should preside over any liturgical celebration where the people are gathered. This is done not to increase the external solemnity, but rather to show the mystery of the Church in a more vivid light (18).

7. Even if the bishop does not celebrate the Eucharist, he may preside at the Liturgy of the Word and the concluding rite (18).

8. In the assembly gathered for the celebration of the liturgy, especially when the bishop presides, each person has a role that depends on the diversity of offices and ministries in the Church. Each person should carry out all and only those parts of the liturgy that pertain to his or her office. Thus, the Church is so manifested in the diversity of its offices and ministries that the individual members constitute one body (19).

Priests

9. Priests should always be present to assist the bishop during liturgical celebrations and should concelebrate with him when he celebrates Mass. Priests are to do only that which is proper to their office. However, when there are no deacons present, they may carry out the diaconal functions but are to vest only as priests (21, 22).

Deacons

10. The deacon holds first place among the ministers. He assists the bishop during the celebration: he proclaims the gospel; announces the inten-

tions of the prayer of the faithful; at the altar, he assists with the book and the chalice; he gives directions to the congregation as necessary (23, 25).

11. In the absence of lesser ministers, he carries out their functions as necessary (25).

12. Ordinarily, three deacons assist the bishop during the Stational Mass: one proclaims the Gospel and ministers at the altar, the other two act as the bishop's assistants (chaplains) (26).

13. If there are a number of deacons present, they may divide up the various diaconal functions among themselves. One of the deacons should take responsibility for the active participation of the faithful. It is also appropriate that one of the deacons function as the master of ceremonies (26).

Acolytes

14. A sufficient number of acolytes (at least seven) are required for an episcopal liturgy. They exercise their ministry even if ministers in a higher order are present (27). They serve as the cross bearer, candle bearers (either two or seven), thurifer, and as the special ministers to the bishop (book bearer, miter bearer, and pastoral staff bearer) (28; see also 125c).

15. When instituted acolytes are present, they should exercise their ministry and distribute the various functions among themselves. They may also distribute the Eucharist, according to the norms of law. When there are no instituted acolytes present, or at least not a sufficient number, their functions may be fulfilled by others who have not been instituted (28).

Reader

16. At celebrations with the bishop, instituted readers should proclaim the readings. If there are several readers present, they should distribute the readings among themselves. In the absence of instituted readers, others may do the readings (30, 31).

17. The reader proclaims the readings before the Gospel. When there is no psalmist or cantor, the reader recites the psalm before the readings. In the absence of a deacon, the reader announces the intentions of the general intercessions (31).

Psalmist

18. The psalmist or cantor sings the psalm between the readings and the Alleluia or Lenten acclamation (33).

Master of Ceremonies

19. The master of ceremonies sees to it that episcopal celebrations are carried out with decorum, simplicity, and order. He has the responsibility of preparing and directing the ministers, as well as the whole ceremony (34).

20. He must be expert in the sacred liturgy, its laws and its pastoral celebration (34).

21. During the celebration, he must exercise the greatest discretion in speech and action and not take the place of the deacons at the side of the bishop (35).

22. The master of ceremonies vests in alb or cassock and surplice. If the master of ceremonies is a deacon, he vests in alb and stole (and dalmatic) (36).

Sacristan

23. The sacristan has the responsibility for the objects used in liturgical celebrations: books, vestments, etc. The sacristan should take care to see that all the things used for the liturgy be kept clean and in good condition (37, 38).

Schola and Musicians

24. All who have a particular responsibility for singing and for providing music for the liturgy (i.e., choir master, cantors, organist, or others) should be aware of and observe the requirements of the liturgical books regarding music (39).

25. Special care should be taken to observe the norms regarding the participation of the congregation in the music of the liturgy (40).

26. During Lent and celebrations for the dead, the organ should be used only to sustain singing. This is also true from after the Gloria on Holy Thursday until the Gloria at the Easter Vigil (41).

27. During Advent, musical instruments should be used in moderation (41).

III.

THE CATHEDRAL CHURCH*

28. The cathedral is the church that contains the bishop's cathedra (chair), a symbol of his teaching authority as the shepherd of a particular church and a symbol also of the unity of belief in the Church's faith, which the bishop proclaims as the pastor of the flock (42).

29. The cathedral ought to be the center of the liturgical life of the diocese. The ordering and decoration of the cathedral should be an example to the other churches of the diocese (44, 46).

Cathedra

30. In the cathedral, there is to be only one cathedra (bishop's chair), which is fixed in its place and so arranged that the bishop may be seen to preside over the whole community of the faithful. The number of steps leading up to the cathedra depends on the structure of the church and should allow the bishop to be seen easily by the faithful. The cathedra is used by the diocesan bishop or by a bishop to whom he has granted its use. The seat for a priest celebrant should be prepared in a place different from the cathedra (47). (Mention is no longer made of the use of the faldstool.)

Tabernacle

31. It is recommended that, in keeping with ancient tradition, the tabernacle in the cathedral church be located in a chapel attached to the main body of the church (49). However, if it happens that the tabernacle is fixed on the altar at which the bishop is to celebrate, the Blessed Sacrament is to be transferred to another worthy place during the celebration (49).

---

*For various aspects of liturgy celebrated in cathedral churches, see the collection of essays edited by the Secretariat of the Bishops' Committee on the Liturgy and the Center for Pastoral Liturgy of The Catholic University of America, *The Cathedral: A Reader* (Washington, D.C.: United States Catholic Conference, Office of Publishing and Promotion Services, 1979).

Presbyterium

32. The presbyterium is the place where the bishop, presbyters, and ministers exercise their ministry. It should be distinguished from the body of the church by its elevation or by its particular structure or decoration, so that it might show the hierarchical office of the ministers by its arrangement. It should be of sufficient size to allow the sacred rites to be easily seen and carried out (50).

33. There should be seats in the presbyterium for concelebrants, priests who do not concelebrate, deacons, and other ministers (50). However, ministers not wearing sacred vestments, the cassock and surplice, or other approved vesture should not enter the presbyterium during sacred celebrations (50).

Secretarium

34. The secretarium is a room placed near the entrance to the cathedral, where the bishop, concelebrants, and ministers vest. The entrance procession begins from the secretarium (53).

35. Ordinarily, the secretarium should be distinct from the sacristy, the place that is used for the storage and preparation of those things necessary for the celebration of the liturgy. On ordinary days, the celebrant and other ministers may prepare for the celebration in the sacristy. (If the cathedral does not have a secretarium, the sacristy or another suitable place may be used instead) (53).

IV.

GENERAL NORMS CONCERNING
EPISCOPAL LITURGIES

Introduction

36. The Second Vatican Council teaches that the rites of the Church should be distinguished by a noble simplicity. This is also true of the liturgical celebrations of the bishop, although the reverence due to him should not be neglected. Jesus Christ is present in the midst of the people in the person of the bishop, and from him as high priest, the life of the faithful in some way depends and is derived (55).

37. When the various orders of the Church participate in the liturgical celebrations of the bishop, its mystery is clearly manifested and in it charity and mutual honor should shine forth among the members of the mystical body of Christ. Thus, even in the liturgy, the Church is led to put into effect the apostles' precept: "Anticipate each other in showing respect" (55).

Vestments and Insignia

Liturgical Vestments and Insignia of the Bishop

38. The bishop wears the same vestments as a priest for liturgical celebrations. In accord with ancient tradition, it is appropriate that he also wear the dalmatic, which is always white, under the chasuble for more solemn occasions, such as: ordinations; the blessing of an abbot or abbess; the dedication of a church or altar; the Stational Mass of the bishop (56). (The dalmatic, when used by the bishop, should be of such size, shape, and material as to appear as a true vestment and not like the flimsy *tunicles* of the past.)

39. In addition to the liturgical vestments, the bishop uses the following insignia of his order: ring; pastoral staff (crozier); miter; pectoral cross; pallium (for archbishops) (57).

40. *Ring:* The ring is always worn by the bishop as a token of faith and as a sign of the marriage bond that exists between him and the local Church (58). (There is no longer any mention of a special ceremonial ring. Since gloves are no longer used, the ring need not be expandable.)

41. *Pastoral Staff:* The staff is a sign of the bishop's pastoral office and is used by him in his diocese. However, any bishop who celebrates solemnly may use the staff with the consent of the local bishop. Only the bishop who presides over a celebration uses the staff when there are many bishops present (59).

The staff is held by the bishop with the curved part toward the people. The staff is ordinarily used in procession; while listening to the Gospel; while giving the homily; during the reception of vows, promises, or a profession of faith. It is also used when the bishop blesses persons, unless he is required to lay hands upon them (59).

42. *Miter:* The miter may be either plain or ornate. However, only one miter is used for any particular celebration. (No mention is made of the linen miter which may be considered a form of the plain miter) (60).

The miter is used while the bishop is seated; while preaching; when greeting the people; while giving brief introductions or instructions (unless it is to be removed immediately after); when he solemnly blesses the people; when he carries out sacramental gestures; when he walks in procession (60).

The miter is not worn for the introductory rites at Mass; for prayers; the general intercessions; the eucharistic prayer; the reading of the Gospel; for hymns which are sung standing; for processions with the Blessed Sacrament or relics of the holy Cross; before the Blessed Sacrament exposed (60).

It is not necessary for the bishop to use the miter and staff when he goes only a short distance from one place to another (60).

43. *Pectoral Cross:* The pectoral cross is worn, suspended from a green cord intertwined with gold threads, under the chasuble (dalmatic) or cope, but over the mozzetta (61). (The practice of wearing the pectoral cross over the chasuble is not sanctioned by the *Ceremonial* and, in fact, is contraindicated.)

44. *Pallium:* Residential archbishops who have received the pallium from the Roman Pontiff wear it over the chasuble within the territory under their jurisdiction when they are celebrating a Stational Mass or at least on some great solemnity. The pallium is also worn for ordinations, the blessing of an abbot or abbess, the consecration of virgins, and the dedication of churches and altars (62).

45. *Archiepiscopal Cross:* Once an archbishop has received the pallium, he may use the archiepiscopal cross when he goes to the church for the celebration of a liturgical function. The image of Christ should face forward (62).

Choir Dress

46. The choir dress of the bishop, both within and outside his diocese, consists of the purple cassock; the purple silk sash with silk fringes (not tassels); the rochet of linen or some similar material; the purple mozzetta

(without the little hood); the pectoral cross, worn over the mozzetta and suspended from a green cord intertwined with gold threads; the purple zuchetto; the purple biretta with a purple pompon (63). Purple stockings may be worn with the purple cassock or even, if desired, with the red-trimmed black cassock (63).

47. *Cappa Magna:* The cappa magna, without ermine, may be used within the diocese on very solemn occasions (64). (Its use is not obligatory and should be reserved only for very special occasions.)

Signs of Reverence

Bows

48. There are two types of bows:
    a. *bow of the head*—this is done at the names of Jesus, Mary, or the saint in whose honor the Mass or the Liturgy of the Hours is being celebrated;
    b. *bow of the body (or deep bow)*—this is made to the altar if the Blessed Sacrament is not present on it; to the bishop; before and after incensing; and as required by the liturgical books (68).

Genuflection

49. The genuflection on the right knee is reserved for the Blessed Sacrament, either exposed or reserved in the tabernacle, and to the cross from the solemn liturgy of Good Friday until the beginning of the Easter Vigil (69).
50. Those who carry objects being used in the liturgical celebration (e.g., cross, candles, *Book of Gospels*) neither bow nor genuflect (70).

Reverence to the Gospel

51. All stand and face the reader for the proclamation of the Gospel at Mass, celebrations of the Word, and at protracted vigil celebrations (74).
52. When the deacon solemnly carries the *Book of Gospels* to the lectern, he is preceded by the thurifer and the acolytes with lighted candles (74). After the deacon announces the Gospel, he incenses the book three times (center, left, right) and proclaims the Gospel. At the conclusion of the Gospel he carries the *Book of Gospels* to the bishop to kiss, or he may kiss it himself (74).
53. When there is no deacon, a priest reads the Gospel; he asks for and receives the blessing of the bishop before proclaiming the Gospel (74).

Reverences to the Bishop

54. Ministers and others who come before the bishop for some purpose make a deep bow to him when they approach and before they depart. The same is done by those who, for some reason, must pass in front of the bishop (76).
55. When the bishop's cathedra is behind the altar, the ministers bow either to the altar or to the bishop, depending on whether they are approaching the altar or the bishop (77).
56. When the bishop goes to the church for a liturgical celebration wearing choir dress, he may be led there publicly by priests and deacons in choir dress, (cassock and surplice). Alternatively, he may go to the church in a simple manner and be greeted by the clergy at the door (79). In either case, the bishop goes first. If he is an archbishop, he may be preceded by an acolyte carrying the archiepiscopal cross with the image of Christ facing forward.
The priests and deacons, walking two by two, follow the bishop. At the door of the church, the senior priest offers the bishop the holy water sprinkler (unless the sprinkling is to take the place of the penitential rite). The bishop sprinkles himself and the others with him and then goes to pray for a brief time before the Blessed Sacrament. Finally, he goes to the secretarium (or sacristy) to vest (79).
57. The bishop may omit the greeting at the door of the church, the sprinkling with holy water, and the visit to the Blessed Sacrament and go directly to the secretarium (or sacristy), where he is greeted by the clergy (70).
58. In processions, the bishop who presides over the celebration in liturgical vestments walks alone after the priests, his assistants walk a little behind him (81).
59. A bishop who presides or participates in choir dress is assisted by two deacons or priests wearing cassock and surplice (81).

Heads of State and Civic Officials

60. A head of state (in the United States, the president or a governor) who attends the liturgy by virtue of his office is greeted at the door of the church by the bishop, who is already vested. If the head of state is a Catholic, the bishop may offer him holy water, otherwise the bishop greets him and escorts him to his seat, which is placed outside the presbyterium. At the end of the celebration, the bishop greets him as he passes by (82).
61. Other high public officials may be received at the church door by the senior ecclesiastic, who greets them and leads them to their seats. The bishop

may greet the officials during the entrance procession and also as he leaves at the end of the celebration (83).

Incensation

62. Incense is used at the Stational Mass:
    a. during the entrance procession;
    b. for the incensation of the altar at the beginning of Mass;
    c. for the procession and proclamation of the Gospel;
    d. at the incensation of the altar, gifts, cross, bishop, concelebrants, and people;
    e. at the showing of the host and chalice after the consecration (86).
63. At other Masses, incense may be used at any or all of the above times (86).
64. The bishop remains seated as he puts incense into the censer; he blesses the incense with the sign of the cross, saying nothing. The deacon holds the incense boat, assists the bishop, and, after the bishop has blessed the incense, hands him the censer (90).
65. A deep bow is made before and after incensing persons and objects, except for the altar and oblations (91). (A bow is no longer made to the altar and oblations before and after incensing them.)
66. Persons or objects are incensed by three swings of the censer. However, relics of the saints are incensed with only two swings of the censer (92). (No mention is made of doubling the swings of the censer.)
67. The altar is incensed by single swings of the censer as the bishop walks around it. The cross is incensed before the altar if it is on or near it, otherwise, it is incensed as the bishop passes before it (93).
68. The bishop receives an incensation while standing and without the miter unless he is already wearing it. Concelebrants are incensed by the deacon as a group. The people are incensed by the deacon from a suitable place (96).
69. The bishop does not continue with the Mass until the incensation is completed (98).

Sign of Peace

70. When the bishop celebrates Mass, he gives the sign of peace to the two closest concelebrants and to the first deacon immediately after the deacon says, "Let us offer. . . ." Meanwhile, everyone else exchanges the sign of peace. A bishop who presides at the liturgy but does not celebrate gives the sign of peace to his assistants (99-100).
71. A head of state (in the United States, the president or a governor) who attends the liturgy in his or her official capacity is given the sign of peace by the deacon or by one of the concelebrants (102).

The Manner of Holding the Hands

Hands Elevated and Extended

72. It is customary for the bishop or priest to stand while praying in the church, with the hands held somewhat elevated and extended (104).

Hands Extended over Persons or Things

73. The bishop holds his hands extended over the people when giving the solemn blessing and as often as required for the celebration of the sacraments and sacramentals, as indicated in the liturgical books (105).

74. At Mass, the bishop and concelebrants hold their hands extended over the offerings during the epiclesis before the consecration. At the consecration, while the bishop holds the host or chalice in his hands and says the words of consecration, the concelebrants say the words of the Lord and, if it seems appropriate, extend their right hands toward the host and chalice (106).

Hands Joined

75. The bishop holds his hands joined together, unless he is holding the pastoral staff, when he is wearing sacred vestments and is walking to the celebration of a liturgical action. He also holds his hands joined while kneeling to pray, while going to the altar from the cathedra or vice versa, and when it is prescribed by the liturgical books (107).

76. The concelebrants and ministers hold their hands joined together when they move about or stand, unless they are carrying something (107).

Other Ways of Holding the Hands

77. When the bishop signs himself or blesses, he places his left hand on his chest, unless he is holding something. When he is standing at the altar and blesses the offerings or something else with his right hand, he places the left hand on the altar, unless noted to the contrary (108).

78. When the bishop is seated and wearing liturgical vestments, he places the palms of his hands on his knees, unless he is holding the pastoral staff (109).

The Use of Holy Water

79. All who enter the church, by a praiseworthy custom, dip their hands into the holy water font and make the sign of the cross as a reminder of their baptism (110).

80. If holy water is to be offered to the bishop when he enters the church, the senior priest of the church hands the sprinkler to the bishop, who sprinkles himself and those accompanying him. Then the bishop returns the sprinkler (111).

This may be omitted if the bishop enters the church vested and when the sprinkling of holy water is to replace the penitential rite at the Sunday (and Saturday evening vigil) Mass (112).

81. The sprinkling of things that are to be blessed takes place according to the norms of the liturgical books (114).

V.

STATIONAL MASS OF THE DIOCESAN BISHOP

Introduction

82. The preeminent manifestation of the local Church is seen when the bishop, as the high priest of his flock, celebrates the Eucharist in the cathedral church, surrounded by his presbyterate and ministers, with the full active participation by the whole holy people of God (119).

83. This Mass, called the Stational Mass, manifests both the unity of the local Church and the diversity of ministries around the bishop and the holy Eucharist (119). (The term *Stational Mass* has its origins in the ancient Roman practice of the pope solemnly celebrating Mass in the various churches of the city. The remnants of this practice are found in the Stational Masses celebrated in Rome during Lent.)

Consequently, large numbers of the faithful are gathered at it, priests concelebrate with the bishop, deacons minister, and acolytes and readers carry out their duties (119).

84. The Stational Mass is celebrated, especially on major solemnities of the liturgical year, when the bishop consecrates the holy chrism and at the evening Mass on Holy Thursday; on celebrations of holy founders of the local Church or diocesan patrons; on the anniversary of the bishop; on the occasion of great gatherings of the Christian people; and also on the occasion of pastoral visitations (120).

85. The Stational Mass is to be sung in accord with the norms that are given in the *General Instruction of the Roman Missal* (nos. 12, 18, 19, 77, 313) (121).

86. The bishop is usually assisted by three deacons: one who proclaims the Gospel and ministers at the altar; two who assist the bishop. If there are many deacons present, they may distribute the various diaconal functions among themselves, and at least one of them should have the responsibility for ensuring the active participation of the faithful. If true deacons are not able to be present, their ministry may be carried out by priests who, vested according to their order, concelebrate with the bishop even if they are bound to celebrate another Mass for the pastoral good of the faithful (122).

87. Bishops and priests who are present at the Stational Mass but do not concelebrate vest in choir dress (123).

Preparations

88. For the celebration of the Stational Mass, the following items are to be prepared:
  a. *in the presbyterium:*
    ○ *Sacramentary;*
    ○ *Lectionary for Mass;*
    ○ booklets for the concelebrants;
    ○ texts of the general intercessions for the bishop and deacon;
    ○ hymnals;
    ○ chalice(s) of sufficient size, covered with a veil;
    ○ (flagon of wine, if needed);
    ○ (pall);
    ○ corporal;
    ○ purificators;
    ○ pitcher, basin, and towel(s);
    ○ vessel of water to be blessed (when used in place of the penitential rite) and holy water sprinkler;
    ○ patens for the communion of the faithful;
  b. *in a convenient place in the church:*
    ○ bread, wine, and water (and other gifts);
  c. *in the secretarium (sacristy):*
    ○ *Book of Gospels;*
    ○ censer and incense boat;
    ○ processional cross;
    ○ seven (or at least two) candlesticks with lighted candles.
89. The following are also to be prepared in the secretarium (sacristy):
  a. *for the bishop:*
    ○ pitcher, basin, and towel;
    ○ (amice), alb, (cincture);
    ○ pectoral cross;
    ○ stole;
    ○ dalmatic;
    ○ chasuble;
    ○ (pallium, for a metropolitan);
    ○ zuchetto;
    ○ miter;
    ○ ring;
    ○ pastoral staff (crozier);

b. *for the concelebrants:*
  - ○ (amices);
  - ○ albs;
  - ○ (cinctures);
  - ○ stoles;
  - ○ chasubles (may be omitted, if necessary);
c. *for the other ministers:*
  - ○ (amices), albs, (cinctures);
  - ○ or cassocks and surplices;
  - ○ or other legitimately approved vestments.

90. The vestments for the Stational Mass are either of the color of the Mass to be celebrated or of a festive color (125).

The Approach and Preparation of the Bishop

91. After the bishop has been formally received at the door of the church, if this has taken place, he goes to the secretarium (sacristy), where he is assisted by the deacons, assistants, and other ministers, who are already vested, to prepare for Mass. He removes his mozzetta and, if desired, the rochet.

After washing his hands, he vests in (amice), alb, (cincture), pectoral cross, stole, dalmatic, and chasuble. If he is an archbishop, the first deacon puts on the pallium over his chasuble. Then, one of the deacons puts the miter on him (126).

92. Meanwhile, the concelebrating priests and the deacons who are not assisting the bishop to vest put on their own vestments (126).

93. When all are ready, the acolyte who is the thurifer goes to the bishop, who puts incense into the censer and blesses it silently with the sign of the cross; a deacon assists the bishop by holding the incense boat. The minister holding the staff then gives it to the bishop. The deacon who will proclaim the Gospel takes the *Book of Gospels,* which he carries closed and in a reverent manner, for the entrance procession (127).

Introductory Rites

94. The entrance procession leaves the secretarium (sacristy) for the presbyterium while the entrance song is sung, in the following order:

  - ○ Thurifer, with smoking censer;
  - ○ An acolyte, carrying the cross (the image of Christ faces forward) between seven or at least two acolytes, carrying candlesticks with lighted candles;
  - ○ Clergy (two by two);
  - ○ Deacon carrying the *Book of Gospels;*

○ Readers (the *Ceremonial* neglects to mention the place of the readers in the procession, however, this seems to be their proper place);

○ Other vested deacons (if present), two by two;

○ Priest concelebrants (two by two);

○ The bishop, who walks alone, wearing the miter and carrying the pastoral staff in his left hand and blessing the people with his right hand;

○ The two deacons who assist the bishop, walking slightly behind the bishop;

○ The ministers of the book, miter, and pastoral staff (128).

95. If the procession should pass before the Blessed Sacrament chapel, there is to be no stop or genuflection (128).

96. The processional cross is placed near the altar. The candles are placed near the altar, on the side table, or in another suitable place in the presbyterium. The *Book of Gospels* is placed on the altar by the deacon who carries it (129).

97. On entering the presbyterium, all bow deeply to the altar, then, the deacons and concelebrants go to the altar, kiss it, and go to their places (130).

98. When the bishop comes before the altar, he hands the pastoral staff to the minister, removes his miter, and makes a deep bow to the altar along with his deacons and ministers. He goes to the altar and, together with the deacons, kisses it (131).

If necessary, incense is again placed in the censer by the acolyte. The bishop, accompanied by the deacons, then incenses the altar and cross (131).

99. After the incensation, the bishop and his ministers go to the cathedra by the shortest route (131).

The two assistant deacons stand near either side of the cathedra so as to be ready to assist the bishop. In the absence of deacons, two of the concelebrating priests fulfill this function (131).

100. All remain standing and make the sign of the cross as the bishop, facing the people, makes the sign of the cross and says, "In the name of the Father" (132).

Greeting and Penitential Rite

101. The bishop extends his hands and greets the people, saying, "Peace be with you," or one of the other formularies in the *Sacramentary*. Then, the bishop, a deacon, or one of the concelebrants may briefly introduce the Mass of the day. Afterwards, the bishop introduces the penitential rite. He concludes the penitential rite with the absolution, "May almighty God." The book bearer holds the *Sacramentary* before the bishop (132).

102. When the third form of the penitential rite is used, the invocations may be made by the bishop, a deacon, or another suitable minister (132).

Blessing and Sprinkling with Holy Water

103. On Sunday (and at the Saturday evening vigil Mass), the penitential rite may be replaced by the blessing and sprinkling with holy water (133).

104. After the greeting, a minister stands before the bishop with a vessel of water to be blessed. The bishop invites the people to pray and, after a brief period of silent prayer, says one of the prayers of blessing. Where it is the custom, salt may be blessed and mixed with the water (133).

The bishop then receives the sprinkler from the deacon and sprinkles himself, the concelebrants, ministers, clergy, and people. He may walk through the body of the church as he sprinkles the people; meanwhile, a suitable song is sung (133).

105. The bishop then returns to his cathedra and, at the conclusion of the song, extends his hands and says the concluding prayer. Then, if prescribed, the *Glory to God* is sung or recited (133).

Kyrie

106. The *Kyrie* is sung or said after the penitential rite, unless the sprinkling with holy water or the third penitential rite was used, or the rubrics for the particular celebration state otherwise (134).

Glory to God

107. The *Glory to God* is sung or recited according to the rubrics. The bishop, one of the concelebrants, or cantors may begin it. All stand during this hymn (135).

Opening Prayer

108. The bishop then invites the people to pray. With hands joined, he sings or says, "Let us pray" (or the longer invitation to prayer found in the *Sacramentary*). After a brief period of silent prayer, the bishop extends his hands and says the Opening Prayer. The book bearer holds the *Sacramentary* before the bishop for the prayer. The bishop joins his hands as he says the conclusion of the prayer, "Through our Lord . . . for ever and ever." And the people respond, "Amen" (136).

Liturgy of the Word

109. The bishop sits after the Opening Prayer and, ordinarily, receives the miter from one of the deacons. All present sit. The deacons and other

ministers are seated in the presbyterium in such a way that they are clearly seen as not having the same rank as the priests (136).

First Reading

110. After all are seated, the reader goes to the lectern. All listen as the reader proclaims the first reading. At the end of the reading, the reader sings or recites, "This is the Word of the Lord," and all respond, "Thanks be to God" (137).

Responsorial Psalm

111. The reader returns to his or her place. After a period of silence, the psalmist, cantor, or the reader sings or says the responsorial psalm, as is indicated in the *Lectionary for Mass*, no. 20 (138).

Second Reading

112. The second reading is proclaimed in the same manner as the first reading (139).

Alleluia

113. The *Alleluia* or Lenten acclamation is then sung. All stand at the beginning of the *Alleluia*, except for the bishop (140).

Gospel

114. The thurifer comes before the bishop, and one of the deacons assists the bishop with the incense boat. The bishop places incense into the censer and blesses it, saying nothing (140).

115. The deacon who is to proclaim the Gospel bows deeply before the bishop and asks for his blessing in a quiet voice, saying, "Father, give me your blessing" (140). The bishop blesses him, saying, "The Lord be in your heart. . . ." The deacon makes the sign of the cross and responds, "Amen" (140).

116. The bishop removes the miter and stands for the proclamation of the Gospel (140).

117. The deacon, accompanied by the thurifer with the smoking censer and two acolytes with lighted candles, goes to the altar. After bowing to the altar, the deacon reverently takes the *Book of Gospels* and, without any reverence to the altar, solemnly carries the *Book of Gospels* to the lectern; he is preceded by the thurifer and acolytes (140).

118. At the ambo, the deacon, with hands joined, greets the people and

then introduces the reading. He first signs the book, then he signs his forehead, lips, and breast. The bishop then takes his pastoral staff. The deacon incenses the book and proclaims the Gospel. All stand and face the deacon during the proclamation of the Gospel.

119. At the conclusion of the Gospel, the deacon carries the book to the bishop, who kisses the book and quietly says, "Through the words." Meanwhile, the deacon and other ministers return to their places. The *Book of Gospels* is carried to the side table or some other suitable place (141). (After the Gospel is proclaimed, the *Book of Gospels* should be treated with the same reverence it received at the beginning of Mass.)

Homily

120. All then sit for the homily. The bishop, wearing the miter and holding the pastoral staff, sits in his cathedra and gives the homily. (In practice, it may be more convenient not to hold the pastoral staff while preaching at the cathedra.) The homily may also be given from another, more suitable, place where the bishop can be seen and heard by all. The homily may be followed by a period of silence (142).

Profession of Faith

121. If a sacramental or consecratory rite or a blessing is to be celebrated after the homily, the norms of the *Pontifical* or *Roman Ritual* are followed. Otherwise, after the homily, the bishop removes the miter and hands his staff to the minister. All rise and sing or say the Profession of Faith, according to the rubrics (143).

122. At the words, "By the power of the Holy Spirit . . . became man," all bow; on Christmas and the feast of the Annunciation, all genuflect (143).

General Intercessions

123. After the Profession of Faith, the bishop stands at the cathedra and, with hands joined, says the invitation to the general intercessions. One of the deacons, or a cantor, reader, or another person offers the intentions from the ambo or another suitable place. The people respond to each intention. After the last intention and its response, the bishop extends his hands and says the concluding prayer (144).

Liturgy of the Eucharist

Preparation of the Altar and Gifts

124. After the general intercessions, the bishop sits and puts on the

miter; the congregation is also seated. The offertory song is then begun and continues at least until the gifts are placed on the altar (145).

125. The deacons and acolytes place the corporal, purificator, chalice, and *Sacramentary* on the altar, and the gifts are then brought forward.

126. It is appropriate that the faithful manifest their participation by bringing forward the bread and wine for the celebration of the Eucharist. Other gifts for the needs of the Church and the poor may be included in the procession with the bread and wine. The deacon(s) or the bishop receives the offerings at a suitable place (e.g., at the cathedra or before the altar). The deacons bring the bread and wine to the altar, while the other gifts are put in a suitable place (145).

127. The bishop then goes to the altar, removes his miter, and receives the paten from the deacon. He holds it in both hands, slightly elevated over the altar, while he quietly says the proper prayer. He then places the paten with the bread on the corporal (146).

128. Meanwhile, the deacon pours a sufficient amount of wine and a small amount of water into the chalice, saying quietly, "By the mystery." Afterwards, he presents the chalice to the bishop, who holds it with both hands, slightly elevated above the altar, while quietly saying the required prayer. He then places it on the corporal. If necessary, the deacon may cover the chalice with a pall (147).

129. If communion is to be distributed under both kinds, or if there are a large number of concelebrants, a flagon(s) of wine is prepared by the deacon and placed on the corporal when the chalice is prepared.[1]

130. After placing the chalice on the altar, the bishop bows at the center of the altar and quietly says, "Lord God, we ask you" (148).

Incensation

131. The thurifer then goes to the bishop. The deacon assists the bishop with the incense boat, and the bishop puts incense into the censer and blesses it. The bishop receives the censer from the deacon and then incenses the offerings. Then, assisted by the deacon, the bishop incenses the altar and cross, as at the beginning of Mass. After this has been done, all stand. The deacon then stands at the side of the altar and incenses the bishop, who stands without the miter.

The deacon next incenses the concelebrants and then the people. The bishop should not give the invitation, "Pray, brethren" or say the Prayer over the Gifts until the incensations have been completed (149).

---

[1]See the norms issued by the National Conference of Catholic Bishops, *This Holy and Living Sacrifice: Directory for the Celebration and Reception of Communion under Both Kinds* (Washington, D.C.: United States Catholic Conference, Office of Publishing and Promotion Services, 1985), nos. 39-42.

132. After the bishop has been incensed, he stands at the side of the altar, without the miter. The ministers come to him with the pitcher, basin, and towel, and he washes and dries his hands, saying, "Lord, wash away." If desired, one of the deacons may remove the bishop's ring while he washes his hands. The bishop then reassumes his ring and goes to the center of the altar (150).

Prayer over the Gifts

133. The bishop faces the people and, extending and joining his hands, invites the people to pray, saying, "Pray, brethren" (151).

134. After the people's response, "May the Lord," the bishop extends his hands and sings or says the Prayer over the Gifts. At its conclusion, the people respond, "Amen" (152).

135. After the Prayer over the Gifts, the deacon removes the bishop's zuchetto and gives it to a minister. The concelebrants come to the altar and stand around it so as not to impede the carrying out of the rites or the view of the faithful (153).[2]

136. The deacons stand behind the concelebrants so that one of them may minister at the chalice or *Sacramentary*. No one should remain between the concelebrants and bishop or the concelebrants and the altar (153).

Eucharistic Prayer

137. The bishop then begins the eucharistic prayer. He extends his hands and sings or says, "The Lord be with you." When he continues, "Lift up your hearts," he raises his hands. With hands extended he adds, "Let us give thanks to the Lord our God." After the response of the people, the bishop continues with the preface. At its conclusion, he joins his hands and, together with the concelebrants, ministers, and people, he sings, "Holy, holy, holy Lord" (154).

138. The bishop then continues with the eucharistic prayer, according to the directives of the *General Instruction of the Roman Missal* (nos. 171-191) and the rubrics of each eucharistic prayer. Those parts of the prayer that are recited by all the concelebrants are said with hands extended and in a quiet voice so that the bishop's voice may be clearly heard by all present.

139. In Eucharistic Prayers I, II, and III, after the words "for N., our Pope," the bishop adds, "and me your unworthy servant" (155). In Eucharistic Prayer IV, after the words "N., our Pope," the bishop adds, "me your unworthy servant" (155).

140. If the chalice and ciborium are covered, the deacon uncovers them before the epiclesis (155).

---

[2]See the guidelines of the Bishops' Committee on the Liturgy in *Study Text V: Eucharistic Concelebration* (Washington, D.C.: United States Catholic Conference, Office of Publishing and Promotion Services, 1978), pp. 24-27.

141. One of the deacons puts incense into the censer and incenses the host and chalice when the bishop shows them to the people (155).

142. The deacons remain kneeling from the epiclesis until after the showing of the chalice (155). After the consecration, the deacon may, if desired, cover the chalice and ciborium once again. The bishop says, "Let us proclaim . . . ," and the people make the acclamation (155).

143. Particular intercessions are inserted in the eucharistic prayer, especially in the celebration of a sacramental or consecratory rite or blessing, according to the structure of each eucharistic prayer, using the texts contained in the *Sacramentary* or other liturgical books (156).

144. The oil for the sick is blessed during the Chrism Mass, according to the rite in the *Roman Pontifical*. The blessing takes place during Eucharistic Prayer I before the bishop says, "Through Christ our Lord you give us," or before the doxology of the other eucharistic prayers, "Through him, with him, in him." For pastoral reasons, the blessing may take place after the Liturgy of the Word (157).

145. The deacon stands next to the bishop and elevates the chalice while the bishop elevates the paten with the host during the final doxology of the eucharistic prayer, until the people sing, "Amen." The final doxology is sung or said by the bishop alone or by the bishop together with the concelebrants (158).

Lord's Prayer

146. The bishop, with hands joined, then says the invitation to the Lord's Prayer, which is sung or recited by all. The bishop and concelebrants sing or recite the Lord's Prayer, with hands extended (159).

147. The bishop alone, with hands extended, says the prayer, "Deliver us, Lord. . . ." All respond with the acclamation, "For the kingdom" (160).

Sign of Peace

148. The bishop says the prayer, "Lord Jesus Christ," and, at its conclusion, faces the people and announces, "The peace of the Lord." The people respond, "And also with you." One of deacons may then give the invitation to exchange the sign of peace; he faces the people and says, "Let us offer. . . ." The bishop gives the sign of peace to at least two of the concelebrants near him and then to the first of the deacons. All in the assembly, according to the custom of the place, may signify peace and charity to their neighbors (161).

Breaking of the Bread

149. Then, the breaking of the bread begins and is continued by some

44

of the concelebrants; meanwhile, the *Lamb of God* is repeated as often as necessary while the bread is being broken. The bishop drops a particle of the bread into the chalice while quietly saying, "May this mingling" (162). (The deacons fill additional chalices, if needed, from the flagon of consecrated wine, either at the altar or at the side table.)

Communion

150. The bishop says the prayer before communion quietly; he then genuflects and takes the paten. The concelebrants, one after the other, approach the bishop, genuflect, and take the Body of Christ. They hold the host in the right hand, which is supported by the left hand, and then return to their places. Alternatively, they may remain in their places and there take the Body of Christ from the paten (163).

151. The bishop then takes the host and, holding it slightly raised over the paten, faces the people and says, "This is the Lamb of God. . . ." He then joins the concelebrants and the people in saying, "Lord, I am not worthy. . ." (163).

152. The communion song is begun while the bishop receives the Body of Christ (163).

153. After the bishop has received the Blood of Christ, he hands the chalice to one of the deacons and then distributes communion to the deacons, ministers, and the faithful (164).

154. Each of the concelebrants approaches the altar and receives the Blood of Christ. The deacons assist the concelebrants and wipe the chalice with the purificator after the communion of each concelebrant (164).

155. After the distribution of communion, one of the deacons drinks the remainder of the Blood of Christ and takes the chalice(s) to the side table, where he immediately purifies and arranges it. Alternatively, this may be done after Mass. Another deacon or one of the concelebrants brings any remaining hosts to the tabernacle and then purifies the paten or ciborium over the chalice at the side table before it is purified (165).

Thanksgiving after Communion

156. When the bishop returns to the cathedra after communion, he puts on his zuchetto and, if necessary, washes his hands. All then may be seated for a period of sacred silence; a hymn of praise or a psalm may be sung (166).

Prayer after Communion

157. Afterwards, the bishop stands at the cathedra, with a minister holding the book before him, or goes to the altar with the deacons, and sings or says, "Let us pray." This may be followed by a brief period of silence,

unless this has already taken place. Then, with hands extended, he sings or says the Prayer after Communion. At the end of the prayer, all respond, "Amen" (167).

Concluding Rites

Announcements

158. If there are any brief announcements, they are made immediately after the Prayer after Communion (168).

Blessing

159. The bishop receives the miter, extends his hands, and greets the people, saying, "The Lord be with you." The people respond, "And also with you." One of the deacons may say, "Bow your heads," or he may use other suitable words. The bishop then solemnly blesses the people, using one of the formularies contained in the *Sacramentary*, the *Roman Pontifical*, or *Roman Ritual*. He holds his hands extended over the people while he says the invocations or the Prayer over the People. The people respond, "Amen," to each of the invocations or the Prayer over the People. The bishop then takes the staff and says, "May almighty God bless you," and makes the sign of the cross three times over the people as he says, " + the Father, + and the Son, + and the Holy Spirit" (169).

160. The bishop may also give the blessing, using one of the formularies described below. However, when he gives the apostolic blessing, according to the norms of law, it replaces the usual blessing of the Mass. The deacon announces the giving of the apostolic blessing, and the bishop gives it with the proper formulary (see nos. 1122-1126 of the *Ceremonial of Bishops*) (169).

Dismissal

161. After the blessing, one of the deacons dismisses the people, saying, "The Mass is ended. Go in peace," or one of the other formularies in the *Sacramentary*. All respond, "Thanks be to God."

162. The bishop, ordinarily, then kisses the altar and makes the required reverence before it. The concelebrants and all others in the presbyterium reverence the altar, as at the beginning of Mass, and return in procession to the secretarium (or sacristy) in the order in which they came (170).

163. When they arrive at the secretarium (or sacristy), all bow, along with the bishop, to the cross. Then, the concelebrants bow to the bishop and unvest in the designated place. The ministers also bow to the bishop and then

put away the things used for the celebration. After they finish unvesting, they leave (170).

Other Masses Celebrated by the Bishop

164. Even when the bishop celebrates Mass with a small gathering of the people and clergy, the celebration should be so arranged as to be an act of the local diocese. It is fitting that he concelebrate with the parish priests or religious communities (171).

165. The bishop should be assisted by a vested deacon. If there is no deacon present, a priest reads the Gospel and assists at the altar; if he does not concelebrate, he vests in an alb and stole (172).

166. The Mass is celebrated as described in the *General Instruction of the Roman Missal*, nos. 77-152 (173).

167. In addition to the usual vestments, the bishop wears the pectoral cross and zuchetto; he may also use the miter and pastoral staff (173).

168. At the beginning of the Mass, the bishop greets the people, saying, "Peace be with you" or "The grace of our Lord" or "The grace and peace" (173).

169. The Gospel is read by a deacon. In the absence of the deacon, a priest may read the Gospel, who, even if he concelebrates, asks for and receives the bishop's blessing. After the Gospel, the *Book of Gospels* is brought to the bishop to kiss, or the deacon or priest kisses it himself (173).

170. Before the preface, the deacon gives the bishop's zuchetto to a minister (173).

171. In Eucharistic Prayers I, II, and III, after the words "for N., our Pope," the bishop adds, "and for me your unworthy servant." In Eucharistic Prayer IV, after the words "N., our Pope," the bishop adds, "me your unworthy servant" (173).

172. At the end of Mass, the bishop blesses the people in the manner described in nos. 1120-1121 in the *Ceremonial of Bishops* (173).

173. A bishop who is not the ordinary of the place may celebrate using the cathedra and the pastoral staff, with the consent of the diocesan bishop (174).

Mass at Which the Bishop Presides
without Celebrating the Eucharist

174. It has been both the doctrine and the traditional teaching of the Church that the bishop should preside over the Eucharist in his communities. It is especially fitting that he should be the celebrant of the Eucharist when he is present at Mass (175).

175. However, if for just reasons he attends Mass without celebrating, he should preside over the celebration and at least celebrate the Liturgy of the Word and bless the people at the end of Mass. This especially applies to the eucharistic celebrations in which some sacramental rite, consecration, or blessing is to take place (175).

176. In these cases, the celebration takes the following form. After the reception of the bishop (as at the Stational Mass), he vests in the secretarium or another suitable place. He wears an alb, pectoral cross, stole, and a cope of suitable color; he also ordinarily uses the miter and pastoral staff. Two deacons (or at least one), vested according to their order, assist the bishop. In the absence of deacons, the bishop is assisted by priests wearing copes (176).

177. The bishop, accompanied by his deacons and ministers, follows the celebrant or concelebrants in the procession to the altar (177).

178. When they come to the altar, the celebrant or concelebrants make a deep bow; if the Blessed Sacrament is reserved in the presbyterium, they genuflect. They then go to the altar, kiss it, and go to their assigned seats (178).

179. The bishop hands the staff to the minister, removes his miter, and, along with the deacons and ministers, bows deeply to the altar (unless, as indicated above, there is to be a genuflection). He then goes to the altar and kisses it (178).

180. If incense is used, the bishop is assisted by the deacons as he incenses the altar and cross in the usual way (178).

181. Then, accompanied by his deacons, the bishop goes to the cathedra by the most direct route. The deacons stand at either side of the cathedra so as to be ready to assist the bishop (178).

182. Everything is done as at a Stational Mass, until the end of the Liturgy of the Word. If a sacramental rite, consecration, or blessing is to be celebrated, the particular norms regarding the profession of faith and the general intercessions should be kept in mind (179).

183. After the general intercessions or the celebration of the sacramental rite, consecration, or blessing, the bishop sits and receives the miter. The deacon and the ministers then prepare the altar in the usual way. If the offerings are brought forward by the faithful, they are received by either the bishop or the celebrant. Then, the celebrant makes a deep bow to the bishop and goes to the altar, where he begins the eucharistic liturgy according to the Order of Mass (180).

184. If incense is used, the bishop is incensed after the celebrant. He removes the miter and rises for the incensation. (If there is no incensation, he stands after the "Pray, brethren" and remains standing at the cathedra up to the epiclesis of the eucharistic prayer) (181).

185. From the epiclesis, through the showing of the chalice, the bishop kneels, facing the altar. A kneeler is prepared for the bishop, either before

the cathedra or in another more suitable place. After the showing of the chalice, he returns and stands at the cathedra (182).

186. After the invitation of the deacon, "Let us offer . . . ," the bishop gives the sign of peace to the deacons on either side of him (183).

187. If the bishop is to receive communion, he goes to the altar and receives the Body and Blood of the Lord after the celebrant (183).

188. During the distribution of communion to the faithful, the bishop may be seated. He stands for the Prayer after Communion, which he says either at the cathedra or the altar. After the prayer, the bishop blesses the people as described in nos. 1120-1121 of the *Ceremonial of Bishops*. After the blessing, one of the assistant deacons dismisses the people (184).

189. The bishop and celebrant kiss the altar at the end, as usual. After the required reverence to the altar, all leave in the same order as they came (185).

190. If the bishop does not preside in the manner described above, he participates in the Mass, vested in mozzetta and rochet. He does not sit in the cathedra, but in another more suitable place (186).

VI.

BLESSINGS GIVEN BY THE BISHOP

191. At the end of the Stational Mass, the bishop blesses the people in the manner described in no. 169 of the *Ceremonial of Bishops* (1118).

192. In other Masses and liturgical actions (for example, at the end of Morning Prayer or Evening Prayer, the end of a procession in which the Blessed Sacrament is not carried, etc.), or even outside liturgical actions, the bishop may give the blessing, using one of the two following formularies (1119).

First Form

193. The bishop receives the miter, if he uses it, and extends his hands and greets the people, saying, "The Lord be with you." Then, he extends his hands over the faithful to be blessed, and continues:

May the peace of God which is beyond all understanding
keep your hearts and minds in the knowledge and love of God and
of his Son, our Lord Jesus Christ.

And all respond, "Amen."

Then, the bishop receives the pastoral staff, if he uses it, and says, "May almighty God bless you," and, making the sign of the cross over the people, he adds, "+ the Father, + and the Son, + and the Holy Spirit." All respond, "Amen."

Second Form

194. After the bishop has greeted the people, as described above, he says, "Blessed be the name of the Lord." All respond, "Now and for ever." Then, the bishop adds, "Our help is in the name of the Lord," and all respond, "Who made heaven and earth." Then, the bishop says, "May almighty God bless you, + the Father, + and the Son, + and the Holy Spirit." All respond, "Amen" (1120).

51

Apostolic Blessing

195. The bishop may impart the apostolic blessing with the plenary indulgence three times a year in his diocese, on the solemn feasts that he designates, even if he only assists at Mass (1122).

196. Other prelates who are equivalent in law to diocesan bishops, even though they have not been ordained to the episcopate, may impart the papal blessing with the same indulgence from the time they begin their pastoral office. They may do this in their territory three times a year, on the solemn feasts they designate (1122).

197. The apostolic blessing is given at the end of Mass in place of the customary blessing. The penitential rite at the beginning of Mass is adapted so as to prepare for the blessing (1122).

198. The bishop introduces the blessing with its plenary indulgence, which will be given at the end of Mass, in the introduction to the penitential rite. He invites the people to repent of their sins and to dispose themselves to participate in this indulgence (1123).

199. In place of the formulary that customarily concludes the penitential rite, the bishop says the following:

May blessed Mary, ever virgin,
the holy apostles Peter and Paul,
and all the saints
assist you with their merits and prayers.

May the almighty and merciful Lord forgive you
and free you from all your sins.

May he help you persevere in fruitful penance,
good example, and sincere charity,
and lead you to everlasting life.

All respond, "Amen" (1123).

200. The general intercessions should always contain an intercession for the Church and one for the Roman Pontiff (1124).

201. After the Prayer after Communion, the bishop receives the miter. The deacon then announces the blessing in these or similar words:

The Most Reverend Father, N., by the grace of God and the Apostolic See, Bishop of this holy Church of N., will give the (apostolic) blessing with a plenary indulgence, in the name of the Roman Pontiff, to all present who are truly penitent and have confessed their sins and received Holy Communion.

Pray to God for our Most Holy Father, Pope N., our Bishop, N.,
and for holy Mother Church and strive, by holiness of life, to walk
in full communion with it (1125).

Then, the bishop stands, wearing the miter and extending his hands, and
greets the people, saying, "The Lord be with you." All respond, "And also
with you."

The deacon may give the invitation, "Bow your heads and pray for God's
blessing," or he may use other suitable words.

The bishop uses one of the formularies for the solemn blessing in the
Sacramentary. He extends his hands over the people as he says the blessing.
He then receives the pastoral staff and concludes the blessing with this for-
mulary:

Through the intercession of the blessed apostles
    Peter and Paul,
may almighty God bless you,
+ the Father, + and the Son, + and the Holy Spirit.

All respond, "Amen."

While he says the latter words, he makes the sign of the cross over the
people (1126).

VII.

ORDINATIONS

202. The ordination of deacons, priests, and bishops is to take place on a Sunday or a feast, unless pastoral reasons would suggest another day (491).

203. The ordination is to take place during Mass, celebrated according to the stational rite. Ordinations are generally celebrated in the cathedral, but, for pastoral reasons, they may be celebrated in another church or oratory (492).

204. According to custom, the actual rite of ordination takes place at the cathedra. However, it may be celebrated in front of the altar or at some other more suitable location for the sake of the participation of the faithful (492).

205. Seats for those to be ordained are prepared in a place that is visible to the faithful during the liturgical action (493).

206. Outside those days listed in numbers 1-4 on the "Table of Liturgical Precedence," and on feasts of the apostles, the Mass in which holy orders are conferred is ordered in the following manner:

a. The entrance and communion antiphons are taken from the ritual Mass for the conferral of orders.

b. The presidential prayers are taken from the appropriate ones in the *Sacramentary,* "Masses and Prayers for Various Needs and Occasions: For the Bishop; For Priests; For the Ministers of the Church."

c. The readings are taken from the *Lectionary for Mass,* nos. 770-774.

d. The preface for the Chrism Mass may be used at the ordination of priests, unless a proper preface is required.

e. The proper intercession for the newly ordained is said during the the eucharistic prayer; the formula given in the *Missal* is used (494).

207. If the ritual Mass for holy orders is not used, one of the readings may be taken from those given for holy orders in the *Lectionary for Mass* (494).

The Ordination of Deacons

208. Those to be ordained vest in (amice), alb, (and cincture). A stole and a dalmatic are also prepared for each candidate. The vestments may be of the color of the Mass, white, or of a festive color (495).

209. Besides those things that are needed for the celebration of a Stational Mass, the following are to be prepared:

a. *Roman Pontifical;*

b. a seat for the bishop if the ordination does not take place at the cathedra;

c. a chalice of sufficient size for communion under both kinds (496).

210. The candidates walk before the deacon who carries the *Book of Gospels* (497). The Mass is celebrated in the usual manner through the Gospel. After the proclamation of the Gospel, the *Book of Gospels* is returned to the altar, where it remains until the presentation of the *Book of Gospels* during the rite of ordination (498).

211. After the Gospel, the bishop is seated at his cathedra or in another seat that has been prepared for him and receives the miter (499). Those to be ordained are called by the deacon in this manner: "Let those to be ordained," and as soon as each candidate is called by name, he answers, "Present," and stands before the bishop, to whom he makes a reverence (500). When all have come before the bishop, a priest deputed by the bishop presents them as is indicated in the *Pontifical*. The bishop concludes, saying, "We rely on the help," and all respond, "Thanks be to God," or give assent to the election in some other manner as determined by the Conference of Bishops (501).

212. Then, when all are seated, the bishop, wearing the miter and holding the pastoral staff (unless he decides not to use them), gives the homily, in which he takes his start from the texts of the sacred Scriptures that were just read, and speaks to the people and to the elect about the office of deacons. He may use either the words of the *Pontifical* or his own words. If there are candidates who will exercise their ministry in the celibate state, he speaks to them about the importance and significance of sacred celibacy in the Church (502).

213. After the homily, the candidates for the presbyterate, as well as the unmarried candidates for the diaconate who are to publicly assume celibacy, rise and, when called by the deacon, come before the bishop, who speaks to them using the admonition in the *Pontifical* or his own words (503).

214. Then, the candidates who are to manifest their intention to commit themselves to celibacy respond, "I am," when the bishop questions them, or by some external sign determined by the Conference of Bishops (504). The bishop concludes, saying, "May the Lord help you . . . ," and the elect respond, "Amen" (504).

215. Then, the other candidates chosen for the diaconate who are not bound to sacred celibacy come forward. The bishop questions all the elect who stand before him, using the text in the *Roman Pontifical* (505). Then, the bishop gives his pastoral staff to a minister, and each of the elect comes to the bishop, kneels before him, and places his joined hands between the hands of the bishop (506).

216. The bishop asks each candidate to make the promise of obedience, according to the formula given in the *Pontifical* (506).

217. If the rite of placing joined hands between the hands of the bishop does not seem appropriate, the Conference of Bishops may make other provisions (506).

218. Then, the bishop removes his miter and, along with all present, rises. He stands, facing the people, with joined hands, and says the invitation, "Let us pray." The deacon then says, "Let us kneel," and immediately the bishop kneels before his own seat; the elect prostrate and all others present kneel at their places (507).

During the Easter season and on Sundays, the deacon does not say, "Let us kneel." Nevertheless, the elect prostrate while the others remain standing (507).

219. The cantors then begin the Litany of the Saints. The names of other saints, for example, patrons or titulars of the church, founders, and patrons of those who are to be ordained, may be added in the proper place. Other suitable invocations, adapted to the particular circumstances, may also be added since the Litany of the Saints takes the place of the general intercessions (507).

220. At the conclusion of the litany, the bishop alone rises and, with hands extended, says the prayer, "Lord God, hear our petitions. . . ." At the conclusion, the deacon says, "Let us stand" (if he invited them to kneel for the litany), and all rise (508).

221. Each of the elect approaches the bishop, who stands at his seat wearing the miter, and kneels before him. The bishop lays hands on the head of each one, saying nothing (509).

222. Then, the bishop removes his miter and, with the elect kneeling before him, sings or says the prayer of consecration, with hands extended (510).

223. At the conclusion of the prayer of consecration, the bishop sits and receives the miter. The newly ordained rise, and deacons or priests vest the new deacons with stoles, worn in the diaconal manner, and dalmatics. Meanwhile, Psalm 84 or another suitable song may be sung; the song continues until all those who have been ordained are vested in dalmatics (511).

224. The newly ordained, now vested as deacons, go to the bishop and kneel before him. He hands each one the *Book of Gospels,* saying, "Receive the Gospel of Christ" (512).

225. Next, the bishop gives the kiss of peace to each of the ordained, saying, "Peace be with you." The newly ordained each respond, "And also with you" (513).

If circumstances allow, other deacons may give the newly ordained the kiss of peace as a sign of their union with them in the order of deacons; meanwhile, Psalm 146 or another suitable song is sung (513).

226. The creed is said, according to the rubrics. However, the general intercessions are omitted (514).

227. The Liturgy of the Eucharist is celebrated according to the Order of Mass. Some of the newly ordained carry the offerings to the bishop for the celebration of Mass; one of the new deacons ministers to the bishop at the altar (515).

228. The newly ordained are commemorated in the eucharistic prayer; the formula given in the *Sacramentary* is used (516).

229. The newly ordained deacons communicate under both kinds. The deacon who assists the bishop administers the cup, and some of the deacons help the bishop in the distribution of communion (516).

230. The parents and relatives of the newly ordained may receive communion under both kinds (in the United States, all present may receive communion under both kinds) (516).

231. The concluding rites follow in the usual manner (517).

The Ordination of Priests

232. All priests are to concelebrate with the bishop at their Mass of ordination. The bishop may allow other priests present to concelebrate with him. In this case, the priests who are ordained take first place among the priest concelebrants (518).

233. Those to be ordained vest in (amice), alb, (cincture), and diaconal stole. In addition, chasubles are prepared for each of those to be ordained. The vestments may be of the color of the Mass, white, or of a festive color (519).

234. Besides those things that are needed for the celebration of a Stational Mass, the following are to be prepared:

　　a. *Roman Pontifical;*

　　b. stoles for the nonconcelebrating priests who will impose hands;

　　c. linen gremiale;

　　d. Holy Chrism;

　　e. those things that are necessary for the washing of the bishop's hands, as well as those of the ordained;

　　f. a seat for the bishop if the ordination does not take place at the cathedra;

　　g. chalice of sufficient size for the communion of the concelebrants and others who are to receive in this manner (520).

235. In the entrance procession, those to be ordained follow the other deacons and precede the concelebrating priests (521).

236. The introductory rites and the Liturgy of the Word, up to the Gospel inclusive, follow in the usual manner (522).

237. After the Gospel, the rite of ordination of priests begins. The bishop is seated at his cathedra or in another seat that has been prepared for him and receives the miter (523).

238. Those to be ordained are called by the deacon in this manner: "Let those who are to be ordained priests," and as soon as each one is called by name, he answers, "Present," and stands before the bishop, to whom he makes a reverence (524).

239. When all have come before the bishop, a priest deputed by the bishop presents them, as indicated in the *Pontifical*. The bishop concludes, saying, "We rely on the help," and all respond, "Thanks be to God," or give assent to the election in some other manner, as determined by the Conference of Bishops (525).

240. Then, when all are seated, the bishop, wearing the miter and holding the pastoral staff (unless he decides not to use them), gives the homily, in which he takes his start from the texts of the sacred Scriptures that were just read, and speaks to the people and to the elect about the office of presbyter. He may use either the words of the *Pontifical* (no. 14) or his own words (526).

241. After the homily, the elect stand before the bishop, who questions them together, as indicated in the *Pontifical* (527).

242. Then, the bishop gives his pastoral staff to a minister, and each of the elect comes to the bishop, kneels before him, and places his joined hands between the hands of the bishop. The bishop asks of each one the promise of obedience, according to the formula given in the *Pontifical*.

If the rite of placing joined hands between the hands of the bishop does not seem appropriate, the Conference of Bishops may make other provisions (528).

243. Then, the bishop removes his miter and, along with all present, rises. He stands, facing the people, with joined hands, and says the invitation, "My dear people." The deacon then says, "Let us kneel," and immediately the bishop kneels before his own seat; the elect prostrate and all the others present kneel at their places.

During the Easter season and on Sundays, the deacon does not say, "Let us kneel." Nevertheless, the elect prostrate while the others remain standing.

244. The cantors then begin the Litany of the Saints. The names of other saints, for example, patrons or titulars of the church, founders, patrons of those who are to be ordained, may be added in the proper place. Other suitable invocations, adapted to the particular circumstances, may also be added since the Litany of the Saints takes the place of the general intercessions (529).

245. At the conclusion of the litany, the bishop alone rises and, with hands extended, says the prayer, "Hear us, Lord our God." At the conclusion, the deacon says, "Let us stand" (if he invited them to kneel for the litany), and all rise (530).

246. Each of the elect approaches the bishop, who stands at his seat wearing the miter, and kneels before him. The bishop lays hands on the head of each one, saying nothing (531).

247. The priest concelebrants and all other priests present (each vested

in a stole worn over an alb or a cassock and surplice) lay hands on the head of each of the elect, saying nothing. After the imposition of hands, the priests remain around the bishop until the prayer of consecration is finished (532).

248. The bishop then removes his miter and, with the elect kneeling before him, sings or says the prayer of consecration, with hands extended (533).

249. At the conclusion of the prayer of consecration, the bishop sits and receives the miter. The newly ordained rise, and the other priests return to their places. Meanwhile, some of them remain to arrange the stoles of the newly ordained as they are worn by priests and to vest them in chasubles (534).

250. The bishop then receives the linen gremial and anoints the palms of each of the newly ordained, who kneel before him, with sacred Chrism, saying, "The Father anointed." Then, the bishop and the newly ordained wash their hands (535).

251. While the newly ordained are being vested in stoles and chasubles, and while the bishop anoints their hands, the hymn *Veni Creator* or Psalm 110 with its antiphon, as given in the *Pontifical,* or another suitable song is sung. The song continues until all the newly ordained have returned to their places (536).

252. Then, the faithful bring forward the bread on the paten and the chalice containing wine and water for the celebration of Mass. The deacon receives them and brings them to the bishop, who hands them to each of the newly ordained who kneel before him, saying, "Accept from the holy people of God" (537).

253. Next, the bishop gives the kiss of peace to each of the newly ordained, saying, "Peace be with you," and the newly ordained each respond, "And also with you." If circumstances allow, other priests present may give the newly ordained the kiss of peace as a sign of their union with them in the order of priests; meanwhile, Psalm 100 with its antiphon or another suitable song is sung. The song continues until all have received the kiss of peace (538).

254. The creed is said, according to the rubrics. However, the general intercessions are omitted (539).

255. The Liturgy of the Eucharist is celebrated according to the Order for the Concelebration of Mass; the preparation of the chalice is omitted (540).

256. The newly ordained are commemorated in the eucharistic prayer; the formula given in the *Sacramentary* is used (541).

257. The parents and relatives of the newly ordained may receive communion under both kinds (in the United States, all present may receive communion under both kinds) (541).

258. The concluding rites follow in the usual manner (542).

60

The Ordination of a Bishop

259. It is especially fitting that the ordination of a bishop take place in his cathedral church. In this case, the apostolic letters are presented and read, and the newly ordained bishop is seated in his cathedra, as noted in the *Ceremonial of Bishops*, nos. 573 and 589 (563).

260. The principal consecrator must be assisted by at least two other consecrating bishops, who concelebrate the Mass with him and the bishop-elect; but, it is fitting for all bishops present, together with the principal consecrator, to ordain the bishop-elect (564).

261. It is most appropriate for all the consecrating bishops and the priests assisting the bishop-elect to concelebrate the Mass with the principal consecrator and the bishop-elect. If the ordination takes place in the bishop-elect's own church, some priests of his own diocese should also concelebrate.

262. Care should be taken that a distinction between the bishops and priests be manifested by their seating (565).

263. Two priests assist the bishop-elect (566).

264. The principal consecrator and concelebrating bishops and priests wear the vestments required for Mass. The bishop-elect wears all the priestly vestments, the pectoral cross, and the dalmatic.

265. If the consecrating bishops do not concelebrate, they wear the alb, pectoral cross, stole, and, if desired, the cope and miter. If the priests assisting the bishop-elect do not concelebrate, they wear the cope over the alb or cassock and surplice.

266. The vestments may be of the color of the Mass, white, or of a festive color (567).

267. Besides those things that are needed for the concelebration of a Stational Mass, the following are prepared:

    a. *Roman Pontifical;*

    b. copies of the consecratory prayer for the consecrating bishops;

    c. linen gremial;

    d. Holy Chrism;

    e. ring for the bishop-elect;

    f. pastoral staff and miter for the bishop-elect;

    g. chalice of sufficient size for the communion of the concelebrants and others who are to receive in this manner (568).

268. The ring, pastoral staff, and miter may be blessed at a convenient time prior to the ordination, as described in the *Pontifical* (569).

269. Seats for the principal consecrator, consecrating bishops, the bishop-elect, and concelebrating priests are arranged as follows:

    a. For the Liturgy of the Word, the principal consecrator should sit at the cathedra or bishop's chair, with the consecrating bishops near the chair. The bishop-elect sits between the assisting priests in an appropriate place within the presbyterium.

b. The ordination should usually take place at the bishop's chair; or, to enable the faithful to participate more fully, seats for the principal consecrator and consecrating bishops may be placed before the altar or elsewhere. Seats for the bishop-elect and his assisting priests should be placed so that the faithful may have a complete view of the liturgical rites (570).

270. When everything is ready, the procession moves through the church to the altar in the usual way. The bishop-elect, between the priests assisting him, follows the priest concelebrants and precedes the consecrating bishops (571).

271. The introductory rites and the Liturgy of the Word, up to the Gospel inclusive, follow in the usual manner (572).

272. If the bishop is ordained in his cathedral church, after the greeting of the people, one of the deacons or priest concelebrants shows the apostolic letters to the College of Consultors in the presence of the chancellor, who records the matter in the acts of the Curia, and he then reads them from the ambo. During the reading of the letters, the congregation is seated; at the end of the reading, all present proclaim, "Thanks be to God," or respond with some other similar acclamation.

273. In newly erected dioceses, communication of these same letters is made to the clergy and people present in the cathedral church by the senior priest (of those present), who records the acts (573).

274. After the proclamation of the Gospel, the deacon returns the *Book of Gospels* to the altar, where it remains until it will be placed on the head of the bishop-elect (574).

275. The ordination of a bishop begins after the Gospel. While all stand, the hymn *Veni Creator Spiritus* is sung, or another hymn similar to it, depending on local custom (575).

276. The principal consecrator and the consecrating bishops, wearing their miters, go to the seats prepared for the ordination and sit (576).

277. The bishop-elect is led by his assisting priests to the chair of the principal consecrator, before whom he makes a sign of reverence. One of the assisting priests asks the principal consecrator to ordain the bishop-elect. The principal consecrator requests that the apostolic mandate be read, while all sit and listen. After the reading, all present say, "Thanks be to God," or give their assent to the choice in some other way, according to local custom (577).

278. Then, the principal consecrator gives the homily, in which he takes his start from the texts of sacred Scripture that were just read, and speaks to the clergy, people, and bishop-elect on the office of bishop. He may use either the words of the *Roman Pontifical* or his own words (578).

279. After the homily, the bishop-elect alone rises and stands before the principal consecrator, who questions him, as is indicated in the *Roman Pontifical*, concerning his resolution to serve the faith and carry out his office (579).

280. Then, the bishops remove their miters and, together with all present,

rise. The principal consecrator stands, facing the people, with hands joined, and says the invitation, "My dear people."

281. The deacon then says, "Let us kneel," and immediately the principal consecrator and consecrating bishops kneel before their seats; the bishop-elect prostrates and all others kneel.

During the Easter season and on Sundays, the deacon does not say, "Let us kneel." Nevertheless, the bishop-elect prostrates while the others remain standing.

282. Then, the cantors begin the Litany of the Saints. The names of the other saints, for example, patrons or titulars of the church, founders, and patrons of the one who is to be ordained, may be added in the proper place. Other suitable invocations, adapted to particular circumstances, may also be added since the Litany of the Saints takes the place of the general intercessions (580).

283. At the conclusion of the litany, the principal consecrator rises and, with hands extended, says the prayer, "Lord be moved. . . ." At the conclusion, the deacon says, "Let us stand," and all rise (581). The bishop-elect rises and goes to the principal consecrator and kneels before him.

284. The principal consecrator receives the miter and lays his hands on the head of the bishop-elect, in silence. Then, all bishops successively come and lay hands on the bishop-elect and remain near the principal consecrator until the end of the prayer of consecration (582).

285. Then, the principal consecrator receives the *Book of Gospels* from one of the deacons and places it open on the head of the bishop-elect; two deacons, standing at either side of the bishop-elect, hold the *Book of Gospels* above his head until the prayer of consecration is completed (583).

286. Then, the principal consecrator removes his miter and, with the consecrating bishops standing near him, also without miters, with hands extended sings or says the prayer of concecration: "God the Father." The part of the prayer from the words, *So now pour* up to the words, *praise of your name* are sung or said by all the consecrators, with hands joined. The remainder of the prayer of consecration is said by the principal consecrator alone. At the end of the prayer, all say, "Amen" (584).

287. At the end of the prayer of consecration, all stand. The principal consecrator and other bishops put on their miters. The deacons close the *Book of Gospels,* which they have been holding above the head of the new bishop. One of them holds the book until it is given to the bishop (585).

288. The principal consecrator puts on the linen gremial, takes the Holy Chrism from one of the deacons, and anoints the head of the bishop, who kneels before him, saying, "God has brought you. . . ." After the anointing, he washes his hands (586).

289. He then receives the *Book of Gospels* from the deacon and hands it to the newly ordained bishop, saying, "Receive the Gospel. . . ." Afterward, the deacon takes the book and returns it to its place (587).

290. Next, the principal consecrator hands the new bishop the pontifical insignia. First, he places the ring on the ring finger of the new bishop's right hand, saying, "Take this ring. . . ." Then, he places the miter on his head, in silence. Lastly, he gives the pastoral staff to the bishop, saying, "Take this staff. . . ."

291. If the new bishop has the use of the pallium, the principal consecrator places the pallium on him before he gives him the miter, using the rite described in no. 1154 of the *Ceremonial of Bishops* (588). All stand. (It is also customary for the pope to confer the pallium personally.)

292. If the ordination takes place in the bishop's own church, the principal consecrator invites him to occupy the cathedra, to which he leads him; if the ordination takes place before the altar, he leads him to another seat. If the new bishop is not in his own church, he is invited by the principal consecrator to take the first place among the consecrating bishops (589).

293. The newly ordained bishop then sets aside his staff, rises, and receives the kiss of peace from the principal consecrator and all the other bishops.

294. After the presentation of the staff, and until the end of the ordination rite, Psalm 96 or any other appropriate song may be sung. The song is continued until all have given the new bishop the kiss of peace (590).

295. If the ordination takes place in the bishop's own church, the principal consecrator may ask the newly ordained bishop to preside over the concelebration of the eucharistic liturgy. If the ordination does not take place in the new bishop's own church, the principal consecrator presides at the concelebration; in this case, the new bishop takes the first place among the other concelebrants (591).

296. The creed is said, according to the rubrics. However, the general intercessions are omitted (592).

297. The Liturgy of the Eucharist is celebrated according to the Order for the Concelebration of a Stational Mass.

298. The newly ordained bishop is commemorated in the eucharistic prayer by one of the concelebrating bishops; the formula given in the *Sacramentary* is used.

299. The parents and relatives of the new bishop may receive communion under both kinds (in the United States, all present may receive communion under both kinds) (593).

300. At the conclusion of the Prayer after Communion, the hymn *Te Deum* is sung, or another hymn similar to it, depending on local custom. Meanwhile, the newly ordained bishop receives the miter and staff and is led by two of the consecrating bishops through the church, as he blesses the people (594).

301. After the hymn, the new bishop may stand at the altar or, if he is in his own church, at the cathedra, and address the people briefly (595).

302. Afterward, the bishop who presided at the Liturgy of the Eucharist

gives the blessing. He stands, facing the people and wearing the miter, and says, "The Lord be with you." Then, one of the deacons may give the invitation for the blessing, and the bishop, with hands extended over the people, gives the invocations of the blessing. Then, he takes the staff and says, "May almighty God," and makes the sign of the cross over the people.

303. The text for the invocation is changed, depending on whether the one who presides is the newly ordained or the principal consecrator (596).

304. After the blessing and the dismissal of the people by the deacon, the procession returns to the secretarium (sacristy) in the customary manner (597).

VIII.

NOTABLE DAYS IN THE LIFE OF THE BISHOP

Ordination of the Bishop

305. Unless legitimately delayed by an impediment, the elect ought to receive episcopal ordination within three months of the receipt of the apostolic letter (1133).

306. The ordination of a bishop takes place during the solemn celebration of Mass, according to the rites and norms described in the *Roman Pontifical* (1134).

307. It is especially appropriate that the ordination of a bishop take place in his cathedral church. In such a case, he takes possession of his diocese at the rite of ordination, during which the apostolic letters are shown and read and the newly ordained is seated in his cathedra (1135).

308. According to the most ancient tradition of the Church, in order to manifest the college of bishops, there should be no fewer than three bishops who, concelebrating, consecrate the bishop, unless the Apostolic See has dispensed from this requirement. It is appropriate that all the bishops present be consecrators (1136).

309. Ordinarily, the principal consecrator of a suffragan bishop is to be the metropolitan, and that of an auxiliary bishop is to be the local bishop, unless it is otherwise provided for by the Roman Pontiff (1137).

Possession of the Diocese

310. Unless legitimately delayed by an impediment, the one promoted to the office of diocesan bishop ought to take canonical possession of his diocese, if he is not already a bishop, within four months after receiving the apostolic letter; if he is already a bishop, he should take possession within two months of its receipt (1138).

311. If the bishop is ordained in his cathedral, he takes possession of the diocese during the rite of ordination, at which time the apostolic letters

67

are shown and read and the newly ordained bishop is seated in his cathedra (1139).

312. If the bishop is transferred from another church or is not ordained in his cathedral, he takes possession of his diocese, within the terms stipulated by law, during the rite of reception at the cathedral. In such a case, the bishop may even take possession of the diocese, for a just reason, by a procurator. Nevertheless, it is preferable that the bishop take possession himself (1140).

Reception of the Bishop in His Cathedral

313. If the Bishop is transferred from another church or does not receive episcopal ordination in his cathedral, the diocesan community is called together for his reception, during the celebration of a Stational Mass, on the occasion when he first comes to his church (diocese) (1141).

314. The bishop is received at the cathedral door by the rector of the cathedral, who is vested in a cope. He offers the bishop a crucifix to kiss and then offers him the holy water sprinkler; the bishop sprinkles himself and then all present. Afterward, he is appropriately led to the Blessed Sacrament chapel, where he kneels in prayer for a short time. He then goes to the secretarium (or sacristy), where all vest for the celebration of the Stational Mass (1142).

315. After the bishop venerates the altar, he goes to the cathedra. At the conclusion of the entrance song, the bishop greets the people and then sits and puts on the miter. One of the deacons or priest concelebrants shows the apostolic letters to the College of Consultors in the presence of the chancellor, who records the matter in the acts of the Curia, and he then reads them from the ambo. During the reading of the letters, the congregation is seated; at the end of the reading, all present proclaim, "Thanks be to God," or respond with some other similar acclamation (1143).

316. Afterward, if the bishop has the right to the pallium, it is placed upon him, according to the rite described in nos. 1147-1155 of the *Ceremonial of Bishops* (1143).

317. Then, according to custom, the bishop is greeted by the rector of the church (1143). Next, according to local custom, some of the clergy and faithful and, if desired, even civil authorities who are present go to the bishop so that they might manifest their obedience and reverence to him (1143).

318. Then, the bishop removes his miter and rises. The penitential rites and, if desired, the *Kyrie* are omitted and the *Glory to God* is sung, according to the rubrics (1143).

319. After the Gospel, the bishop addresses his people for the first time, in the homily. The Mass continues in the customary manner (1144).

320. If the metropolitan leads the bishop into his cathedral, he presents the bishop to the rector, at the door of the church, and he presides at the entrance procession. At the cathedra, the metropolitan greets the people and

requires the apostolic letters to be shown and read. After the reading and the acclamation of the people, the metropolitan invites the bishop to be seated in the cathedra. The bishop then rises, and the *Glory to God* is sung, according to the rubrics (1145).

321. If, however, for a just reason, the bishop takes possession of his diocese by means of a procurator, the rite of reception is celebrated as described above; the showing and reading of the apostolic letters are omitted (1146).

322. From the day of his taking possession, the name of the bishop is inserted in the eucharistic prayer by all priests who celebrate Mass in his diocese, even in the churches and oratories of exempt religious (1147).

323. An auxiliary bishop or coadjutor who was ordained either in the cathedral of his diocese or another place is fittingly presented to the people by the residential bishop, within a liturgical action (1148).

Imposition of the Pallium

324. The imposition of the pallium takes place, whenever possible, during the rite of ordination, immediately after the giving of the bishop's ring and before the miter is placed on the new bishop. The principal consecrator imposes the pallium on the new bishop, saying, "To the glory of almighty God," as given in no. 329 below (1149).

325. Mass is celebrated according to the stational rite. The pallium is carried by one of the deacons in the entrance procession and placed on the altar (1150).

326. A suitable seat is prepared in a worthy place in the presbyterium for the bishop who has been commissioned to bring the pallium from the Apostolic See. He presides at the celebration up to the imposition of the pallium (1151).

327. After the entrance song, the bishop whose office it is to impose the pallium greets the people in the usual manner and briefly explains to them what is about to be done. Then, the deacon, if the giving of the pallium is connected with the reception of the bishop in his cathedral, goes to the lectern and reads the apostolic mandate. All are seated and listen to it and at its conclusion respond, "Thanks be to God" or in some other more suitable manner, according to local custom (1152).

328. After the reading of the apostolic mandate or, if the giving of the pallium does not take place during the reception of the bishop in his cathedral, immediately after the introduction of the one who presides, the elect comes before the bishop who has been commissioned to impose the pallium; he is seated and wears the miter. The elect kneels before the bishop, makes the profession of faith, and takes the oath, according to the form contained in the apostolic letters (1153).

329. Once this has been done, the prelate receives the pallium from the deacon and places it on the shoulders of the elect, saying:

To the glory of almighty God
and the praise of the Blessed Virgin Mary
and the apostles Peter and Paul,
in the name of Pope N., Bishop of Rome,
and of the holy Roman Church,
for the honor of the Church of N.,
which has been placed in your care,
and as a symbol of your authority as metropolitan archbishop,
we confer on you the pallium taken from the tomb of Peter
to wear within the limits of your ecclesiastical province.

May this pallium be a symbol of unity
and a sign of your communion with the Apostolic See,
a bond of love, and an incentive to courage.
On the day of the coming and manifestation
    of our great God and chief shepherd, Jesus Christ,
may you and the flock entrusted to you
be clothed with immortality and glory.
In the name of + the Father, + and of the Son, + and of the Holy
    Spirit.

All respond, "Amen" (1154).

330. The penitential rite and, if desired, the *Kyrie* are omitted. The archbishop who received the pallium then begins the *Glory to God* if it is to be said or sung. The Mass then continues in the usual way (1155).

The Death and Funeral of the Bishop

331. When the bishop is sick or dying, he should give an example to his people by receiving the sacraments of penance and the Eucharist. If he is seriously ill, he should receive the sacrament of the anointing of the sick (1157).

332. When death is near and certain, the bishop should ask for and receive holy viaticum, according to the rite described in *Pastoral Care of the Sick: Rites of Anointing and Viaticum* (1158).

333. The presbyterate, and especially the College of Consultors, should offer spiritual assistance to the bishop before and during his last agony by taking care to recite the prayers of commendation with him and by uniting all the faithful in the diocese in prayer for him (1159).

334. When the bishop dies, they should say the prayers described in the

70

ritual.[1] The body of the bishop is then dressed in purple (or white) vestments as for a Stational Mass. The pastoral staff is not used, but the miter is. If he was an archbishop with the right to use the pallium, he is also vested in it. If the bishop was transferred from other sees and received several pallia, these are placed in the coffin, unless he specified otherwise.

335. When the body is transferred to the cathedral for the celebration of the funeral, it is placed in a suitable place, where the faithful may visit it and pray for him. The vigil service or the Liturgy of the Hours is celebrated at the bier or in the cathedral itself (1160).

336. The clergy and people gather at a suitable time for the celebration of the bishop's funeral at the cathedral. The president of the regional conference of bishops or the metropolitan presides and the other bishops, as well as the priests of the diocese, concelebrate with him (1161).

337. The funeral rites are as described in nos. 821-838 of the *Ceremonial of Bishops* (1162) and are celebrated according to the rites in the *Order of Christian Funerals*.

338. The bishop who is the principal celebrant alone presides at the final commendation (1163).

339. The body of a diocesan bishop is ordinarily buried in the cathedral of his diocese. The body of a bishop who has retired is buried in the cathedral of his last see, unless he has made other provisions (1164).

340. All the communities of the diocese should pray for the deceased bishop by celebrating Mass for him, or the Liturgy of the Hours, or in some other manner. (1165)

The Vacant Episcopal See

341. The administrator of a vacant diocese should invite the clergy and people of the diocese to pray that a pastor may be chosen who will fulfill the needs of the Church. The "Mass for the Election of a Bishop" should be celebrated at least once in all the churches of the diocese, except on those days when it is prohibited (1166).

---

[1] See *Order of Christian Funerals*, approved by the National Conference of Catholic Bishops, November 1985, for the various rites prescribed for the death of a Christian.

APPENDIX I

CONTENTS OF THE
CAEREMONIALE EPISCOPORUM

Decree

Introduction

Part I: Episcopal Liturgy in General
    Chapter 1: The Nature and Importance of Episcopal Liturgy
        I. The Dignity of the Local Church
        II. The Bishop as Foundation and Sign of Communion in the
            Local Church
        III. The Importance of Episcopal Liturgy
        IV. The Bishop's Role of Preaching

    Chapter 2: Offices and Ministries in Episcopal Liturgy
    Chapter 3: The Cathedral
    Chapter 4: General Norms
        Praenotanda
        I. Vestments and Pontifical Insignia
        II. Signs of Reverence in General
        III. Incensation
        IV. The Sign of Peace
        V. The Manner of Extending Hands
        VI. The Use of Holy Water
        VII. The Care of Liturgical Books and the Manner of Proclaim-
            ing Various Texts

Part II: The Mass
    Chapter 1: The Stational Mass of the Diocesan Bishop
    Chapter 2: Other Masses Celebrated by the Bishop
    Chapter 3: Mass at Which the Bishop Presides but Does Not Cele-
            brate the Eucharist

Part III: The Liturgy of the Hours and Celebrations of the Word of God

APPENDIX II

DOCUMENTATION

"On the Use of Pontificals"
Motu Proprio of Pope Paul VI
Pontificalia insignia (21 June 1968)

Pontifical insignia have been created and approved by the Church over the course of the centuries in order to give to the faithful a clear and visible expression of the bishop's sacred office. That expression occurs notably in the solemn presentation of these insignia within the rite of episcopal ordination or consecration by the use of formularies that describe the pastoral charge entrusted to the bishop over his people. Particularly in the Middle Ages, many authors have written treatises on these insignia that bring out both their pastoral and their spiritual symbolism. The pontificals bring out the bishop's rank and power: he is the shepherd and teacher of his people, commanded to guide and to feed them; he is "to be looked on as the high priest of his flock, the faithful's life in Christ in some way deriving from and depending on him."[1]

For several centuries the pontifical insignia belonged exclusively to bishops; gradually, however, they were granted to other ecclesiastics. Some of these were assistants to the bishops in the pastoral ministry; others were prelates, for example, abbots in their monasteries or territories who possessed some jurisdiction exempt from the local bishop; others were clergy, either individually or as a class, who were given some symbol of rank or honor. The result is that today there are many clergy who do not possess episcopal rank yet on various grounds and in different degrees have the privilege of using pontificals. This privilege is regulated by the prescriptions of the *Codex Iuris Canonici*, the Motu Proprio *Inter multiplices* of our predecessor St. Pius X, 21 February 1905, and the Apostolic Constitution *Ad incrementum* of our predecessor Pius XI, 15 August 1934.

The recent Second Vatican Ecumenical Council has, however, shed new light on the dignity and office of bishops in the Church and has brought out more sharply the distinction between bishops and priests of secondary rank.

---

[1]SC art. 41 [DOL 1 no. 41].

Moreover in treating of the liturgy the Council has ruled that "rites should be marked by a noble simplicity . . . they should be within the people's power of comprehension and as a rule not require much explanation."[2] For the elements taken up into the liturgy are signs that point to unseen divine realities;[3] the faithful must therefore be able to grasp them readily and, as far as possible, immediately, in order that they may lead to heavenly things.

In its norms relevant to the reform of the liturgy, the Council was therefore consistent in ruling that "the use of pontifical insignia should be reserved to those ecclesiastical persons who have episcopal rank or some definite jurisdiction."[4] We should take into consideration the mentality and conditions of our own era, which attaches great importance to the authenticity of signs and to the real need that liturgical rites be marked by a noble simplicity. Accordingly it is very necessary to restore authenticity to the use of pontifical insignia as expressions of the rank and the charge of those who shepherd the people of God.

To carry out the intention of the Council, therefore, we decree the following by our apostolic authority, *motu proprio*, and of set purpose.

1.   In conformity with the directives of the Constitution on the Liturgy art. 130, we command that from now on besides bishops only those prelates are to use pontifical insignia who although of nonepiscopal rank have actual jurisdiction, namely:

a. papal legates;

b. abbots and prelates with jurisdiction over a territory separate from any diocese (see CIC can. 319, § 1; can. 325);

c. apostolic administrators with a permanent appointment (can. 315, § 1);

d. abbots regular with jurisdiction, after they have received the abbatial blessing (can. 625).

2.   Even if they do not have episcopal rank, the following are to use pontifical insignia, except for the bishop's chair and staff:

a. apostolic administrators with a temporary appointment (can. 351, § 2, 2°; see also can. 308);

b. vicars and prefects apostolic (can. 308).

3.   The prelates listed in nos. 1 and 2 possess the rights mentioned only within their own territory and during their tenure. Abbots primate and abbots general of monastic congregations during their tenure, however, may use pontificals in all the monasteries of their order or congregation. Other abbots

---

[2]SC art. 34 [DOL 1 no. 34].

[3]See SC art. 33 [DOL 1 no. 33].

[4]SC art. 130 [DOL 1 no. 130].

regular with jurisdiction possess the same right within every monastery of their order, but upon consent of the abbot or conventual prior of that monastery.

4. Blessed abbots regular, once they have ceased their ruling office, and titular abbots may use pontificals within any monastery of their order or congregation, but upon consent of the abbot or conventual prior of that monastery.

5. Other prelates not having episcopal rank who were named before the present Motu Proprio continue to possess the privileges they now enjoy regarding use of certain pontificals, as granted them by law either individually or as members of a class. They may, however, give up such privileges of their own accord, in keeping with the provisions of the law.

6. In view both of the recent decrees of the Council and of the principles already here explained on preserving the authenticity of signs in the liturgy, prelates named in the future will no longer possess the right to use pontificals; those in nos. 1 and 2 are exceptions.

7. What has been said here regarding prelates applies as well to any clergy who use pontificals no matter what their entitlement.

8. The effective date for the matters decreed by this Motu Proprio is 8 September 1968.

Whatever has been laid down by this Motu Proprio we command as settled and ratified, all things to the contrary notwithstanding, even those deserving explicit mention.

"On the Simplification of Pontifical Rites and Insignia"
Instruction of the Sacred Congregation of Rites
Pontificalis ritus (21 June 1968)

Esteem for the pontifical rites and care over them are matters of centuries-old standing. These rites provide a symbol of the honor by which the bishop's dignity is to be acknowledged in the Church and they place clearly before the faithful the mystery of the Church itself.

The *Caeremoniale Episcoporum*, a collection of the norms required for pontifical celebrations made by papal authority, is evidence of the Church's continuing attentiveness regarding rites to be celebrated by a bishop.

The *Caeremoniale* preserves venerable traditions belonging to the ancient celebrations in which priests, deacons, and ministers perform their ministry when a bishop presides and the congregation of the faithful is present. In many places, however, it contains matters that are obsolete and not in keeping with our own times.

Reform of the liturgy was meant to bring the rites once again to a noble simplicity and to authenticity as signs. Once begun many bishops insistently requested that pontifical celebrations and insignia also be simplified.

Not everything in the *Caeremoniale Episcoporum* can be revised before completion of the definitive reform of the Order of Mass, the divine office, and the liturgical year. But careful reflection on the matter led to the conclusion that it is now timely to establish certain measures that, while preserving the dignity of pontifical rites, will also mark them with simplicity. Therefore the following matters are ordered to be changed or introduced at once.

I. PRIESTS AND MINISTERS IN A CELEBRATION WITH THE BISHOP

A. PRIESTS AND MINISTERS IN A CONCELEBRATED MASS

1.   The preeminent manifestation of the Church is most clearly expressed in the eucharist at which the bishop presides, surrounded by his college of priests and ministers, with the people taking an active part. To show this more clearly it is especially fitting, now that concelebration has been restored, for priests to be present with the bishop at a solemn celebration and concelebrate with him, in accord with an ancient tradition in the Church.

So that priests who hold some higher rank may have more opportunity to concelebrate with the bishop:

a. One of the concelebrants may perform the function of assistant priest.

b. When no deacons are present, two of the concelebrants may replace assistant deacons.[1]

B. ASSISTANT PRIEST AND DEACONS

2.   It belongs to the assistant priest to stand by the bishop's side as he reads. When the bishop is not at the altar, however, a server holds the book in front of him.

3.   As a rule, priests of higher rank assist the bishop at the chair. It is permissible, however, for a deacon to do so and to perform the ministries of the assistant deacons; if necessary, the deacon and subdeacon of the Mass may fulfill these functions.

C. DEACONS AND SUBDEACONS

4.   At a celebration with a bishop presiding, the reality of orders and ministries should stand out clearly. Therefore, deacons and subdeacons, if any are present, should not be excluded from serving as the deacon at the altar and the subdeacon for Mass.

5.   Several deacons, clad in their proper vestments, may exercise their ministry, each taking a part of this ministry.

6.   When a bishop celebrates a Mass without singing, it is fitting that he be assisted by at least one deacon, vested in amice, alb, cincture, and stole; the deacon reads the gospel and assists at the altar.[2]

7.   If all the deacons and subdeacons called for by the rubrics are not available on Holy Thursday at the chrism Mass, fewer suffice. If none at all are available, some of the concelebrating priests are to carry the oils.

D. CANONS PRESENT IN CHOIR

8.   At a pontifical Mass of a bishop the canons are always to wear a canon's choral vesture.

E. LESSER MINISTERS

9.   Ministers who assist the bishop at the throne are not to wear a cope.

II. CHAIR OR THRONE OF THE BISHOP

10. The honored and traditional name for the chair of the bishop is the *cathedra*.

---

[1]See *Rite of Concelebration* nos. 18 and 19.

[2]See *Ritus servandus in celebratione Missae* (1965) no. 44.

11. From now on there is to be no baldachin over the bishop's chair; but the valuable works of art from the past are to be preserved with utmost care. Further, existing baldachins are not to be removed without consultation with the commissions on liturgy and art.

12. Depending on the design of each church the chair should have enough steps leading up to it for the bishop to be clearly visible to the faithful and truly to appear as the one presiding over the whole community of the faithful.

13. In all cases there is to be only a single episcopal chair and the bishop who sits on it is the one who is celebrating or presiding pontifically at the celebration. A chair is also to be provided in a convenient place for any other bishop or prelate who may be present, but it is not to be set up as a *cathedra*.

III. SIMPLIFICATION OF SOME OF THE PONTIFICAL VESTURE AND INSIGNIA

14. A bishop who wears an alb as required by the rubrics need not wear the rochet under the alb.

15. Use of the following is left to the bishop's choice:
    a. buskins and sandals;
    b. gloves, which may be white on all occasions if he prefers;
    c. the morse (*formale*) worn over the cope.

16. The following are to be dropped:
    a. the episcopal tunicle previously worn under the dalmatic;
    b. the silk lap-cloth (*gremial*); another gremial is retained, if it serves a purpose, e.g., for the performance of anointings;
    c. the candle (*bugia*) presented to the bishop for readings, unless it is needed;
    d. the cushion for kneeling during the rites.

17. In keeping with ancient tradition, the bishop is to retain the dalmatic when he celebrates solemnly. In addition he is to wear it in a recited Mass at the consecration of a bishop, the conferral of orders, the blessing of an abbot or an abbess, the blessing and consecration of virgins, the consecration of a church and an altar. But for a reasonable cause he may omit wearing the dalmatic under the chasuble.

18. In each liturgical service a bishop is to use only one miter, plain or ornate depending on the character of the celebration.

19. Any bishop who, with the consent of the local bishop, celebrates solemnly may use the episcopal staff.

20. Only a single cross is to be carried in a procession, to increase the dignity of the cross and its veneration. If an archbishop is present, the cross will be the archiepiscopal cross, to be carried at the head of the procession, with the image of Christ crucified facing forward. The recommended practice is to stand the processional cross near the altar so that it serves as the altar cross. It this is not done, the processional cross is put away.

IV. THINGS TO BE CHANGED OR ELIMINATED IN EPISCOPAL RITES

A. PUTTING ON AND TAKING OFF VESTMENTS

21. In any liturgical ceremony a bishop vests and unvests in a side chapel or, if there is none, in the sacristy, at the chair, or, if more convenient, in front of the altar. Vestments and insignia, however, are not to be laid on the altar.

22. When a bishop presides in a side chapel at an hour of the office suited to the time of day, he wears the chasuble right from the start of the office.

B. THE BOOK OF THE GOSPELS

23. The Book of the Gospels, preferably distinct from the book of other readings, is carried by the subdeacon at the beginning of Mass. After the bishop celebrant has kissed the altar and the Book of the Gospels, this is left on the altar at the middle. After saying the prayer, *Almighty God, cleanse my heart*, the deacon takes the Book of the Gospels before asking the bishop's blessing for the singing of the gospel.

C. LITURGY OF THE WORD IN A MASS AT WHICH A BISHOP PRESIDES WITHOUT CELEBRATING

24. When, in keeping with no. 13, a bishop presides at a Mass without celebrating, he may do all those things in the liturgy of the word that usually belong to the celebrant.

D. THINGS TO BE ELIMINATED

25. The bishop is no longer greeted by a genuflection but by a bow. In carrying out their service the ministers stand rather than kneel before him, unless kneeling is more practical.

26. The washing of the bishop's hands within a liturgical rite is carried out by acolytes or clerics, not by members of the bishop's household.

27. All prescriptions in the *Caeremoniale Episcoporum* on forming a circle of assistants in front of the bishop or on certain parts recited in alternation are abolished.

28. Also to be abolished is the previous tasting of the bread, wine, and water prescribed in the *Caeremoniale*.

29. If a bishop presides at a canonical hour before Mass, he omits those preparatory prayers for Mass that the *Caeremoniale* prescribes during the chanting of the psalms [lib. II, cap. viii, no. 9].

30. In a Mass at which a bishop presides without celebrating, the celebrant, not the bishop, blesses the water to be poured into the chalice at the offertory.

31. The bishop may omit use of the miter and staff as he goes from one place to another when there is only a short space between them.

32. A bishop does not use the miter, unless he already has it on, for the washing of the hands and the receiving of incensation.

33. The blessing after the homily mentioned in the *Caeremoniale* is abolished.

34. When, in keeping with the provisions of law, a bishop bestows it, the papal blessing with its formularies replaces the usual blessing at the end of Mass.

35. The cross is not to be brought to an archbishop when he gives the blessing.

36. A bishop is to take the staff before he begins the blessing formulary, so that this is not interrupted. Thus in this instance the raising and extension of the hands prescribed in the *Ritus servandus* no. 87, are omitted.

An archbishop is to put the miter on before the blessing.

37. After the blessing, the bishop, with miter and staff, reverences the altar, as he is leaving. If he has the right to wear the pallium, he does not take it off at the altar but in the sacristy.

V. PRELATES OF LESS THAN EPISCOPAL RANK;
OTHER CLERICS; OTHER LITURGICAL RITES

38. All the points in this Instruction on simplifying pontifical vesture, insignia, and rites and on matters to be eliminated or modified apply in due measure to prelates or clerics of less than episcopal rank who by law or by privilege are entitled to certain pontifical insignia.

39. The suppressions and changes that have been decreed here apply also to all liturgical services celebrated by other clerics.

Pope Paul VI on 10 June 1968 approved this Instruction drawn up by the Congregation of Rites and the Consilium, confirmed it by his authority, and ordered its publication, setting 8 September 1968, the feast of the Birth of the Blessed Virgin Mary, as its effective date.

"On the Vesture, Titles, and Insignia of Cardinals, Bishops, and Lesser Prelates" Instruction of the Secretariat of State *Ut sive sollicite* (31 March 1969)

In conscientious fulfillment of his obligation to watch over the universal Church and in his efforts to carry out the directives and teachings of Vatican Council II, Pope Paul VI has devoted his attention even to the outward symbols of ecclesiastical life. His intention has been to adapt such externals to the altered conditions of the present time and to relate them more closely to the spiritual values they are meant to signify and to enhance.

The issue at hand is disquieting to our contemporaries. It involves harmonizing, without giving in to conflicting, extreme demands, propriety and dignity with simplicity, practicality, and the spirit of humility and poverty. These qualities must above all characterize those who, by their admittance to ecclesiastical office, have received a clear duty of service to the people of God.

Prompted by such considerations, the Pope in the last two years has seen to the issuance of norms on the dress and other prerogatives of cardinals (see SC Ceremonies, Decree, 6 June 1967, Prot. N. 3711), the Motu Proprio *Pontificalis Domus*, 28 March 1968, on the composition of the papal household, the Motu Proprio *Pontificalia insignia*, 21 July [June] 1968, on pontificals,[a] and the related Decree of the Congregation of Rites, Prot. N. R.32/ 968, on the same date.[b]

Pope Paul, however, wished to change even more extensively the regulations on the vesture, titles, and coats-of-arms of cardinals, bishops, and prelates of lesser rank. He therefore ordered a special commission of cardinals and the papal Secretary of State to study the issue thoroughly, taking into account both established custom, contemporary usage, and the spiritual values connected with various symbols of ecclesiastical life, even though they are external nonessentials.

The consultation of this commission is the basis of the present Instruction. In an audience granted to me, the Cardinal Secretary of State, 28 March 1969, Pope Paul VI approved this Instruction and set 13 April 1969, Low Sunday, as its effective date.

All things to the contrary notwithstanding, even those deserving explicit mention.

---

[a]See DOL 549; AAS mistakenly has 21 July 1968 as the date.

[b]See DOL 550 [the document is an instruction, not a decree].

PART ONE
DRESS

1.   The following continue in use: the cassock of red wool or similar material, with sash, piping, buttons, and stitching of red silk; the mozzetta of the same material and color as the cassock but without the small hood.

The *mantelletta* is abolished.

2.   The black cassock with piping and red-silk stitching, buttonholes, and buttons, but without the oversleeves, also continues in use.

The elbow-length cape, trimmed in the same manner as this cassock, may be worn over it.

3.   The sash of red watered-silk, with silk fringes at the two ends, is to be worn with both the red cassock and the red-trimmed black cassock.

The sash with tassels is abolished.

4.   When the red cassock is worn, red stockings are also worn, but are optional with the red-trimmed black cassock.

5.   The dress for ordinary or everyday use may be the plain black cassock. The stockings worn with it are to be black. The red *collare* [rabat or rabbi] and the skullcap of red watered-silk may be worn even with the plain black cassock.

6.   The red watered-silk biretta is to be used only with choral dress, not for everyday wear.

7.   Use of the red watered-silk cloak [*ferraiuolo*] is no longer obligatory for papal audiences and ceremonies held with the pope present. Its use is also optional in other cases, but should always be restricted to particular solemn occasions.

8.   The great cloak of red wool [*tabarro*] is abolished. In its place a decent black cloak, even with cape, may be used.

9.   The red cardinalatial hat [*galero*] and the red plush hat are abolished. But the black plush hat remains in use, to which, when warranted, red and gold cord and tassels may be added.

10.   Use of red shoes and buckles, even silver buckles on black shoes, is abolished.

11.   The rochet of linen or similar material is retained. The surplice or cotta is never to be worn over the rochet.

12.   The *cappa magna*, without ermine, is no longer obligatory; it can be used only outside Rome, on very solemn occasions.

13.   The cord and chain for the pectoral cross are retained. But the cord is to be worn only with the red cassock or sacred vestments.

14. By analogy with what has been laid down for cardinals, bishops keep the purple cassock, the mozzetta without the small hood, and the black cassock with red piping and buttons.

The mozzetta may be worn anywhere, even by titular bishops.

The purple *mantelletta* or cloak is abolished.

The red-trimmed black cassock with its other red ornaments is no longer obligatory as ordinary dress. The small cape may be worn over it.

15. With regard to the sash, stockings, ordinary dress, *collare* [rabat], skullcap, biretta, *ferraiuolo*, cloak [*tabarro*], buckles, rochet, *cappa magna*, cord and chain for the pectoral cross, the rules laid down in nos. 3–8 and 10–13 are to be followed.

16. The black plush hat with green cord and tassels, which is to be the same for all bishops, both residential and titular, is retained.

17. Like all other bishops, those appointed from religious orders and congregations will use the purple cassock and the black cassock, with or without red trimmings.

C. LESSER PRELATES

18. The higher-ranking prelates of the offices of the Roman Curia who do not have episcopal rank, the auditors of the Rota, the promoter general of justice, and the defender of the bond of the Apostolic Signatura, apostolic protonotaries *de numero*, papal chamberlains, and domestic prelates retain the purple cassock, the purple *mantelletta*, the rochet, the red-trimmed black cassock without cape, the purple sash with fringes of silk at the two ends, the purple *ferraiuolo* (nonobligatory), and the red tuft on the biretta.

The silk sash with tassels, purple stockings, and shoe-buckles are abolished.

19. For supernumerary apostolic protonotaries and for honorary prelates of His Holiness, the purple *mantelletta*, the silk sash with tassels, purple stockings, shoe-buckles, and the red tuft on the biretta are all abolished.

The purple cassock, the red-trimmed black cassock without cape, and the silk sash with fringes are retained. If necessary, the unpleated surplice [cotta] may be worn over the purple cassock, in place of the rochet.

The purple *ferraiuolo*, although not obligatory, is retained for supernumerary apostolic protonotaries, but not for honorary prelates of His Holiness.

20. Chaplains of His Holiness keep the purple-trimmed black cassock with purple sash and other ornaments. It is to be worn also in sacred ceremonies.

The purple cassock, the purple *mantellone*, the sash with tassels, and shoe-buckles are abolished.

PART TWO
TITLES AND COATS-OF-ARMS

21. The titles called "titles of kinship," which the pope uses in reference to cardinals, bishops and other ecclesiastics, will be limited to the following: for a cardinal, "Our Esteemed Brother"; for a bishop, "Esteemed Brother"; for others, "Beloved Son."

22. For cardinals the title "Eminence" and for bishops, "Excellency," may still be used and the adjectival phrase "Most Reverend" added.

23. The simple titles "Lord Cardinal" and the Italian *Monsignore* may be used to address a cardinal and a bishop either orally or in writing.

24. "Most Reverend" may be added to the title *Monsignore* in addressing bishops.

25. For the prelates listed in no. 18, "Most Reverend" may also be added to the title *Monsignore*.

For the dean of the Roman Rota and the secretary of the Apostolic Signatura, the title "Excellency" may be used but without "Most Reverend." The same applies to the vice-chamberlain of the Holy Roman Church.

26. For supernumerary apostolic protonotaries, honorary prelates, and chaplains of His Holiness the title *Monsignore*, preceded where applicable by "Reverend," may be used.

27. In formal letters, the expressions "kissing the sacred purple," "kissing the sacred ring" may be omitted.

28. Cardinals and bishops are granted the right to have a coat-of-arms. The use of coats-of-arms must conform to the rules of heraldry and must be simple and clear.

The episcopal staff and the miter in coats-of-arms is suppressed.

29. Cardinals are allowed to have their coats-of-arms affixed to the outside of their titular or diaconal church.

The portrait of the titular cardinal is to be removed from such churches. Inside, near the main door, a plaque is permitted with the name of the titular cardinal inscribed in a manner suited to the style of the building.

ADDITIONAL PROVISIONS

30. With regard to the dress and titles of cardinals and patriarchs of the Eastern rites, the traditional usages of their individual rite is to be followed.

31. Patriarchs of the Latin rite who are not cardinals are to dress like other bishops.

32. Papal legates, whether bishops or not, are to conform to the rules already given for bishops.

But within their own jurisdiction they may use the sash, skullcap, biretta, and *ferraiuolo* of watered silk.

They will be accorded the title "Esteemed Brother" referred to in no. 21, only if they are bishops.

33. Prelates *nullius*, abbots *nullius*, apostolic administrators, vicars and prefects apostolic who are not bishops may dress like bishops.

34. In the matter of forms of address conferences of bishops may lay down suitable rules conforming to local usages, but they are to take into account the norms and rules contained in the present Instruction.

35. Concerning the dress and titles of canons, holders of benefices, and pastors, the Congregation for the Clergy will issue pertinent rules for the future that are in keeping with the reason for this Instruction, namely, to reduce everything in this matter to a simpler form.

"On the Reform of Choral Vesture"
Circular Letter of the Sacred Congregation of Clergy
Per Instructionem (30 October 1970)

The Instruction *Ut sive sollicite*, which the Cardinal Secretary of State issued on 31 March 1969 by order of Pope Paul VI, directed this Congregation for the Clergy to make rules, consistent with that Instruction, for the choral vesture and titles of canons, holders of benefices, and pastors.[1]

This Congregation has consulted the Latin-rite conferences of bishops concerned, compared their decisions, and submitted them to review by the papal Secretariat of State. The Congregation in virtue of the present Circular Letter now entrusts to the same conferences of bishops the task of simplifying choral vesture. They are to be guided by the following universal rules:

1.   This Letter abolishes all, even centuries-old and immemorial privileges, in keeping with the directives of the Motu Proprio *Pontificalia insignia*, 21 June 1968,[2] and the Instruction *Ut sive sollicite*, 31 March 1969.[3]

2.   Only those canons who are bishops may wear the purple mozzetta. Other canons are to wear a black or grey mozzetta with purple trim. Clerics holding benefices are to wear a black or grey mozzetta and pastors are to use only the stole.

3.   Canons, clerics holding benefices, and pastors are also forbidden to use any of the following insignia, which are still in use in some places: the *mantelletta*, the sash with tassels, red stockings, shoes with buckles, purple cloak, rochet, miter, staff, ring, pectoral cross.

4.   Everything in the Apostolic See's documents already mentioned concerning cardinals and bishops applies also, in due proportion, to other categories of ecclesiastics.

Each conference of bishops is given the power to put into effect gradually, while respecting the requirements of law, the aforementioned directives contained in the documents of the Apostolic See and in the present Letter.

---

[1] No. 35 [DOL 551 no. 4532].

[2] See AAS 60 (1968) 374–377 [DOL 549].

[3] See AAS 61 (1969) 334–340 [DOL 551].

"Allowing Use of the Chasuble-Alb"
Concession of the Sacred Congregation for Divine Worship
La Sacrée Congrégation (1 May 1971)

A petition conforming to the General Instruction of the Roman Missal no. 304[a] has been addressed to the Congregation for Divine Worship to authorize wearing of the chasuble-alb with the stole over it in liturgical celebrations. This is a loose-fitting priestly vestment that entirely envelops the celebrant's body and thus replaces the alb.

1. This proposal seems to be consistent with the general principles on liturgical vestments, as determined by the General Instruction of the Roman Missal no. 297.[b] In particular:

a. The prominence given to the stole by reason of its being worn over the chasuble-alb puts due emphasis on the hierarchic ministry of the priest, namely, his role as presiding over the assembly *in persona Christi* (See Introduction no. 4; Text no. 60).[c]

b. Since it is so ample that it covers the celebrant's entire body, the chasuble-alb maintains the sacredness of things used in the liturgy and adds an element of beauty, if it is of graceful design and good material.

2. Taking into account the diversity in pastoral situations, the Congregation for Divine Worship therefore authorizes use of this vestment under the following conditions.

a. For the usual celebration of Mass, particularly in places of worship, the traditional liturgical vestments are to continue in use: the amice (when needed to cover the neck completely), the alb, the stole, and the chasuble, as required by the General Instruction nos. 81 a, 298, and 299.[d] It is preferable to ensure the observance of this prescription, but at the same time not to refuse to meet legitimate needs of the present day.

b. For concelebration, the General Instruction (no. 161)[e] has confirmed the faculty granted to concelebrants, except for the principal concelebrant, to wear just the alb with the stole over it. This makes for a certain simplicity but at the same time respects the dignity and sacredness of the liturgical

---

[a]See DOL 208 no. 1694.

[b]See DOL 208 no. 1687.

[c]See DOL 208 nos. 1379; 1450.

[d]See DOL 208 nos. 1471 and 1688.

[e]See DOL 208 no. 1551.

service. It is proper in concelebrations that the principal concelebrant wear the vestments listed here in no. 2 a.

c. The chasuble-alb may be worn in concelebrations for Masses with special groups, for celebrations outside a place of worship, and for other similar occasions where this usage seems to be suggested by reason of the place or people involved.

d. As to color, the only requirement for use of the chasuble-alb is that the stole be of the color assigned to the Mass.

3. We should add that the approval of a new type of vestment must not put an end to the creativity of artisans and vestment makers regarding the design or the material and color of vestments. But all their efforts must respect the twofold requirement formulated by the General Instruction no. 297[f] and repeated here in no. 1 a and b: to give proper emphasis to the celebrant's ministry and to ensure the sacredness and beauty of the vestments.

---

[f]See DOL 208 no. 1687.

"On the Pallium"
Motu Proprio of Pope Paul VI
Inter eximia episcopalis (11 May 1978)

The pallium, received from the revered tomb of St. Peter,[1] is deservedly included among the special insignia of the bishop's office. It is one of those marks of honor that the Apostolic See has from earliest times accorded to Churches and their heads, first throughout Europe, then throughout the world. The pallium, "a symbol of archiepiscopal power,"[2] "belongs *de iure* only to an archbishop,"[3] since, through its bestowal the fullness of the pontifical office is conferred along with the title of archbishop."[4] As historical records show,[5] however, the popes have continued the early practice of honoring episcopal sees with the dignity of the archiepiscopal pallium as a grant in perpetuity in order to enhance the standing of such Churches because of the renown of the place, the antiquity of the Churches, and their unfailing reverence toward the See of Peter. Furthermore, the popes have also followed the practice of conferring the pallium as a personal privilege to reward the exceptional merits of illustrious bishops.[6]

Vatican Council II, however, has decreed that new and effective norms are to specify the rights and privileges of metropolitans.[7] We have accordingly decided to revise the privileges and practices related to the granting of the pallium in order that it might serve as a distinctive symbol of the power of the metropolitan.[8]

We have received and taken into consideration the opinions of the Roman curial congregations involved and of the commissions for the revision of the code of canon law and of the Eastern code of canon law. Of set purpose and by our own supreme apostolic authority, we now decree that for the entire Latin Church the pallium hereafter belongs exclusively to metropolitans and

---

[1]See PR, pars prima, *ed. typica* (Rome, 1962) 62.

[2]CIC can. 275.

[3]Benedict XIV, *De Synodo dioecesana* lib. 2, 6, no. 1.

[4]Benedict XIV, Ap. Const. *Ad honorandum*, 27 March 1754, § 17.

[5]See Benedict XIV, *De Synodo dioecesana* loc. cit.

[6]See Benedict XIV, Ap. Const. *Inter conspicuos*, 29 Aug. 1744, no. 18.

[7]See CD no. 40: AAS 58 (1966) 694; ConstDecrDecl 318.

[8]See CIC can. 275.

the Latin-rite patriarch of Jerusalem.[9] We abolish all privileges and customs now applying either to particular Churches or to certain bishops as a personal prerogative.

As to the Eastern Churches, we repeal canon 322 of the Motu Proprio *Cleri sanctitati*.[10]

We permit archbishops and bishops who already have received the pallium, however, to use it as long as they continue as pastors of the Churches now entrusted to them.

In the case of the episcopal ordination of a pope-elect who is not yet a bishop, wearing of the pallium is granted by law to the cardinal dean of the college of cardinals[11] or else to that cardinal to whom the rite of ordination is assigned according to the Apostolic Constitution *Romano Pontifici eligendo*.[12]

The effective date for these norms is the date of their publication in the *Acta Apostolicae Sedis*.

We command that whatever has been decreed by this Motu Proprio is ratified and established, all things to the contrary notwithstanding, even those deserving explicit mention.

---

[9]See Pius IX, Apostolic Letter *Nulla celebrior*, 23 July 1947: *Acta Pii IX*, pars. 2, vol. 1, 62.

[10]See AAS 49 (1957) 529.

[11]See CIC can. 239, § 2.

[12]See AAS 67 (1975) 644–645.